JUSTICE

# EARLY AMERICAN
# WOOD CARVING

*Amore et gratia hunc librum dedico*

*Ednae Florantiae, uxori dilectae.*

PLATE I. *Ship's Carving (Stephen Decatur?)*

# EARLY

# AMERICAN

# WOOD CARVING

*by Erwin O. Christensen*

Cleveland  New York

# THE WORLD PUBLISHING COMPANY

FIRST EDITION

*Library of Congress Catalog Card Number: 52-8444*

CC 1052

*Copyright 1952 by The World Publishing Company*
*Manufactured in the United States of America*
*Design & Typography Jos. Trautwein.*

# PREFACE

This volume aims to give the reader a broad view of early American wood carving in the United States from Colonial days to the end of the nineteenth century. The material here illustrated, though known to specialists, is generally unfamiliar and largely unpublished. As an art-historical subject, wood carving has not been dealt with before in book form.

Certain parts of wood carving have been well documented, like Samuel McIntire by Fiske Kimball, William Rush by Henri Marceau, figureheads by Pauline Pinckney and New Mexican bultos by E. Boyd, and by Wilder and Breitenbach. Specialties like butter molds, toys, architectural carving and others have been published in *Antiques*, in the Metropolitan Museum of Art bulletins and elsewhere. Jean Lipman discussed wood carving in connection with folk art, and much has been written about furniture. Basic contributions were made by the researchers during the days of the Government-sponsored projects of the late 1930's. But, with notable exceptions, there is still a dearth of specialized research. The nineteenth century has been neglected; there are no books on shop figures, midwestern religious art or local schools like the carvers of Cincinnati. It has frequently been necessary to use such terms as "presumably," as often information is not available, and may never be available. Fortunately, the material itself constitutes a record and reveals a good deal; such an approach through study and comparison has been used where possible.

For facts on individual items the author is indebted to the research files of the Index of American Design. For works referred to in the text, but not illustrated, Index of American Design reference numbers are given in footnotes. I wish to thank Mrs. Robert Adair Black of Cincinnati and Mary Minot Reed, Librarian of the Cincinnati Art Museum for the use of documents and photographs on Cincinnati wood carvers. I am also grateful to E. Boyd, Curator of the Museum of New Mexico at Santa Fe for information on the New Mexican bultos, and to William L. Warren of Litchfield, Connecticut, formerly Supervisor of the W.P.A. State Project of Connecticut, for his account of his discovery and preservation of circus carvings, the last artistic remnants of "The Greatest Show on Earth." Numerous other persons have helped by giving me information on individual wood carvers. I owe much to my wife, Edna Florance Christensen, for her painstaking editing of the text.

The illustrations are, unless stated otherwise, by courtesy of the Index of American Design of the National Gallery of Art.

*Much credit is due to the artists who made the original Index renderings, from which the illustrations were made. Their names will be found in the list of illustrations.*

# CONTENTS

# LIST OF ILLUSTRATIONS

### COLOR PLATES

Plates I, VIII, XI, XII, courtesy of the *Index of American Design, National Gallery of Art, Washington, D. C.*

Plates II, III, IV, V, VI, VII, IX, X, courtesy of *Fortune Magazine.*

BLACK AND WHITE

ENDPAPERS

# INTRODUCTION

In America, with its vast virgin forests, wood has always been a favored material. Even today our domestic architecture is predominantly wooden, and in Colonial days wood was used for many purposes for which we now use metal, glass or plastics. The early tools, utensils and even machines were of wood; clocks had movements of wood with wheels, gears and pinions cut to a high degree of precision. For every new design for pressed glass, a wooden model was carved, from which the mold was made. Pioneer conditions were unfavorable for a flowering of the major arts, but artistic expression could not be stifled altogether. The number of wood carvers in Early America must have been considerable, and the work turned out was not all of a utilitarian nature.

Nor did the craft, as we may be inclined to believe, come to an end with the introduction of the machine. Even after machine-made articles became available, some crafts and folk arts continued; there were fine wood carvings being created in the eighties and nineties of the last century. In fact, the use of wood in the United States and Canada reached an all-time high during the nineteenth century.

Wood carving developed no single unified style. The country was too large, the population drawn from too many different races; a century was not sufficient to fuse the different developments into any style that we might speak of as characteristically American. We should not regret this lack of an easily recognized American style, for to it is due much of the variety and interest of our art. There were no art frontiers in North America, and it is chiefly for practical reasons that Canadian wood carving is not represented. The subject has been well documented by Marius Barbeau.

Where wood carving is ornamental, as in fine furniture and architecture, it is closer to the European tradition, and yet it achieves an individuality of its own. When wood carving served the needs of the home, of commerce and of business, or was done for pleasure and relaxation, it was closer to a native expression.

Wood carving tends either to academic art, as in the fine craft of furniture carving, or to folk art. To academic art belong those few wood carvers who have absorbed the art tradition of their own period and country, usually through study in an art academy. To folk art belong those who have absorbed this tradition incompletely, or not at all. They were artisans trained in a shop, or they depended on native talent. It is also at times convenient to speak of popular art instead of folk art, giving the term a special connotation. The academic wood carver enters into our subject, as in the case of William Rush; the carver of a fine Chippendale chest we should call a craftsman; the man who worked on wooden Indians might be properly labeled a folk artist. These terms may be loose in their meaning, but they are not interchangeable. Other terms like amateur, non-professional, provincial and even commercial might also be justified in special cases. This variety of terms to describe the carvers is due to the fact that early American wood carving was done by all kinds of people, ranging from the gifted amateur to the trained professional. Much of wood carving is professional (Chapter I through IV), but household articles and related objects (Chapter V) include the work of amateurs.

When we consider the question of traditions and influences we arrive at these conclusions:

The full-length American figurehead no longer constituted an integral part of ship design, as Pauline Pinckney has shown. It was fitted to the bow of the ship and projected beyond its contour. This means it became an accessory before it was eliminated entirely.

Cigar-store figure carving followed figurehead rather than traditional shop-figure carving, and produced a prolific native school of folk carving with incidental academic influences.

A folk art tradition from an earlier eighteenth-century shop-figure manner also continued into the nineteenth century, running parallel to cigar-store figure carving.

An academic influence from William Rush and contemporary marble sculpture continued in nineteenth-century wood carving. Allowance must be made, in nineteenth-century cigar-store figures, for some merging of figurehead, early shop-figure and academic traditions.

A native development occurred in decoys, weathervanes and smaller carvings (Chapter V).

Religious figure carving (Chapter VI) absorbed influences from old Mexico and from French Canada.

Besides the scholarly, objective approach, there is another more personal approach. Is a particular example aesthetically satisfying; does it arouse in us a pleasurable reaction that we can linger over and recall? Aesthetic pleasure is elusive; it is mingled with other interests; it is not always recognized by the individual, and is difficult to put into words. Unlike the pleasures of literature and music, that captivate us and force us under their spell, the pleasures of the visual arts, even of masterpieces, are gentle. We may even have to be conditioned to get satisfaction from looking at a wood carving.

But to stress aesthetics in wood carving is to give the subject an emphasis it rarely had in its own day. Even taking such objects out of their environment for individual analysis isolates them in a way contrary to the purpose for which they were made. And yet that is what has happened to much of the art that has come to us from the past. Symbolic, religious and even practical meanings no longer function in a figurehead, a bulto, or a weathervane, but instead we now prize these objects for their artistic value.

# CHAPTER I

# FIGUREHEADS AND STERNBOARDS

The carved figure for the prow of a ship has always been more than a decoration. In an earlier, more primitive era, a ship required a guardian spirit; a carved dragon to frighten enemies, or a painted eye to enable it to find its way.[1] Perhaps more is involved than superstition on the part of those who manned the ships. A ship is always "she" and since 1726, when British ships were allowed free choice of figureheads, instead of a lion, a ruler or some allegorical subject, the figurehead has often represented a woman. In the days of long and dangerous ocean voyages sailors had personal feelings for the ships on which their lives depended. The figureheads which symbolized those ships may have been symbols for something else, even closer to the sailors' hearts than the ships; they may be unconscious, unrecognized mother-symbols.

The nineteenth-century figureheads represent a last stage in a long development of wood carving applied to sailing vessels. We shall better understand American figurehead carving if we know something of its European background. The period from 1600 to about 1800 in Europe and America represents the maturity of the art of ship carving. During this period, the ship's stern was richly carved, much like a town-house facade; its massive breadth overbalanced the figurehead. The ship had not entirely abandoned the idea of being a house made to float on water.

Even the battleship showed a high stern with gallery above

gallery carved with figures, friezes and a profusion of ornamentation. The very portholes for the cannon were enclosed by carved wreaths; a use of art that seems fantastic when compared to the grimness of modern warfare. To the end of the eighteenth century ship carving reflected the styles of academic art. Renowned sculptors, like Pierre Puget, were commissioned to design the sculptural decorations of ships. Colbert, minister to Louis XIV, was ordinarily eager to have French vessels "carry to foreign shores magnificent testimony of the grandeur of the King of France."[2] But even he had to admit that in the matter of ship carving "Puget had an over-heated imagination and went too far." He advised Puget to restrain himself so as not to hamper the stability of the ship through unnecessary weight.[3]

An excessive load of carved wood interfered with the maneuvering of the ship and endangered its safety. We are told of one captain who, as soon as he got to sea, sawed off his great figures and let them go overboard.[4] On British ships carved work was discontinued in 1796, when the British Admiralty issued an order to leave off carved work from His Majesty's ships.[5] Only the single figureheads and the stern decorations which matched the figureheads and were subordinate to them continued, though reduced in importance, to the end of the sailing-vessel period. Even after the sailing ship had achieved its final functional form in the American clipper, the figurehead remained. But now naval architects were no longer concerned with the ornamentation, and academic sculpture, at least in the United States, ceased to play a part in figurehead design, which was left to folk art. Figureheads were commissioned to craftsmen who designed, carved and installed them but had nothing else to do with the design of the ship.

In 1637 the ornamentation, which meant carving, painting and gilding of the *Sovereign of the Seas*, had cost 6,691 pounds,[6] probably the most lavish expense ever incurred for ship decoration. In 1797 the Skillin brothers of Boston received $719.33[7] for carving the first figurehead of the famous *Constitution*.

When ship carving was so abundant as to overwhelm the vessel, it was rejected by the sailors; after ship carving had developed into a folk art no captain would sail without a figurehead. Probably the reason for this change in attitude was the fact that the single figures of the nineteenth-century ships were more personal, more easily understood and appreciated. They fitted more nearly into the experience of many people. Such had not been the case with the seventeenth-century vessels, where the elaborate sculptural decorations of kings and warriors of history and mythology belonged to a strange world, above the level of the humble sailor.

Anyone who, a century ago, strolled along the water front in one of our harbors,[8] on India Wharf in Boston, on South Street in New York or on Philadelphia's Front Street, would have seen many ships with figureheads and stern carvings, reflecting what was left of the grandeur of the eighteenth century. During its last period the figurehead broadened its appeal by introducing new subjects. With the creation of a new nation, the symbolism of the late eighteenth century was enriched with new contents. Liberty and Columbia appeared; animals and birds, especially eagles, greatly expanded the repertory beyond the lion and dragon of an earlier period. Figures of presidents and of statesmen, as well as characters from literature and history, and men and women who were neither kings nor nobles, took up positions on the prows.

The influence of the Classic Revival of the early nineteenth century shows itself in the choice of Greek or Roman gods or heroes as subjects. A three-quarter-length figurehead of Janus[9] has a double head, one facing forward and one backward. Janus was the Roman guardian deity of gates, who faces two ways as every door looks two ways. A figurehead of Hercules represents a stocky and bearded man wearing a lion's skin. In his uplifted hand he may have held a club.[10]

American Indians furnished the motifs for some figureheads, as one in the Peabody Museum, Salem, Massachusetts, made for the ship *Indian Chief*.[11] Another Indian, with uplifted head and the left arm swung back[12] ended as a tobacconist's figure, but is known to have been a figurehead before about 1850. Figurehead Indians are distinguishable from cigar-store Indians by their characteristic pose, and often by the greater skill shown in the carving of the figure.

Figureheads were not easily discarded; when their careers on one ship came to an end they might be repainted to serve in a new character on another vessel. That must have been the case with a Columbia[13] in the Mariners' Museum at Newport News, Virginia, a three-quarter figure that grows out of a billethead and is believed to be of foreign design. An American flag painted across the top of the billethead looks like a later decoration not originally intended. A serpent around her wrist, and her mournful look, are details that point to the Egyptian queen about to die from the poisonous sting of the asp. Originally the figurehead might have served for some ship named Cleopatra.

Wooden figureheads, like marble statues, have a general as well as an individual style. The massive elaboration of the traditional figurehead style is combined with nineteenth-century realism in Tamanend,[14] figurehead of the U.S.S. *Delaware*. It was carved in 1820 by William Luke of Portsmouth, Virginia. This half-length figure rises out of a scroll and a wreath of ivy. The chief of the Delaware Indians, with arrows and pipe sticking out of his belt, is thoroughly American in subject. The bust is technically accomplished, and still academic rather than in the folk-art manner. Its forceful characterization and its emphasis on anatomy suggest the portrait.

In the bust of Benjamin Franklin[15] the carver had in mind a real person, Franklin in his advanced years. It is realistic in the treatment of hair and eyes and in the difference between bones and muscles. The posture suggests the figurehead, but it is also more academic than one would expect from most figurehead carvers. The bust is by an experienced craftsman and has been attributed to William Rush, perhaps around 1815.

William Rush (1756–1833)[16] was the son of a ship carpenter and like other figurehead carvers he learned his craft as apprentice to a master carver. There were no art schools at that time[17] but casts played a part in the training of American artists, including wood carvers. From 1811 on, annual art exhibitions were held, to which Rush contributed, along with other leading sculptors, painters and architects of the day. Though figurehead carving tended in the direction of folk art, Rush is still linked to the academic tradition. A well-known work is his wood-

carved statue of Washington[18] in Independence Hall, Philadelphia.

Figurehead carvers took suggestions from classic sculpture.
The head may be based on one classic type, the pose on another,
and both may be combined with a toga-like costume. A figurehead for the *Cassandra Adams*,[19] built in 1876, clearly reflects
the pose of the classic marble statue of the Artemis of Versailles.
Though the original had long been in Paris, it was known
through illustrations.

The soft edges and rounded surfaces of the drapery of neo-
classic marbles become sharp in the wooden figureheads. We
see this illustrated in the figurehead from the *White Lady*[20]
(Fig. 1), a vessel not definitely identified, but possibly from
Bath, Maine. The carver has abandoned the classic and developed his own style. The drapery folds might owe something to
a recollection of a breeze blowing them back, but this idea has
not been carried through realistically. Actually, drapery is
made into a pattern; the long lines that descend along the
thighs are allowed to stand as flat bands and sharp ridges. There
is no attempt to imitate cloth, and there is no real classic influence. Working with the grain, the carver arrives at a linear
style that grows out of the use of his tool.

Broad surfaces stand out effectively against undercut portions so that a contrast of light and dark is assured. The arms
are pressed to the body to keep them within the shape of the
tree trunk; the bent forearm is cut from a separate piece but is
kept close to the figure to insure strength. Grooves and depres-
sions are slanted to shed water. There is a sturdy character in
the detail that may look clumsy when the figurehead is detached, but was calculated for its proper effect when set in
place on the ship. When we see the carving in near view we
admire its consistency of style. Features, hair and necklace are
in keeping; small folds recall large ones; the billethead is related to the figure. We have here a remarkable achievement in
folk carving; strong, consistent, in proper scale and in good
taste. The carver evolved this elaboration, probably out of his
own experience, with little conscious dependence on outside
sources; and yet simplicity and bulk are retained in spite of sur-

Fig. 1. *Figurehead from the ship* White Lady, *nineteenth century.*

face elaboration. This figurehead, in the Whaling Museum of New Bedford, is among the best that have survived. Colonel Charles A. L. Sampson of Bath, Maine, has been suggested as the possible carver.

Often the females are sturdy and buxom, hardy and healthy in appearance. A full-length figurehead, Belva Lockwood,[21] named after a leader in the suffrage movement, is a good example; a three-quarter-length from a ship by the name of *Martha*[22] in the Mariners' Museum in Newport News, Virginia, is another, and so is the figurehead from the *Julia Lawrence* (Fig. 2). The *Julia Lawrence* was a vessel of 748 tons, built in Rockland, Maine, about 1856. Though not a large ship, she carried a three-quarter-length figurehead. The carver succeeded in giving to this lady a proud bearing; with raised chin she gazes straight ahead as if her attention were fixed on the distant horizon. The head suggests the portrait; the figure is in the impersonal folk-art manner, more classic than contemporary in costume.

If you have ever looked up at the bow of an old sailing vessel when she stood high in the water, you may remember how small the figurehead looked.[23] Massiveness and roundness were necessary to make it effective. Arms were carved with the grain and remain, as here, within the thickness of the log, so that they are safe from fracture. Actually the carver was by no means free to arrange the arms any way he pleased, but here they look free and natural.

The full-length American figurehead is slightly detached from the line of the hull and often is represented as if stepping forward, head erect, with the wind blowing the drapery. A magnificent example is the figurehead from the *Indian Princess* (see endpaper back) in the Peabody Museum of Salem, Massachusetts. This one is over seven feet high. One owned by the Addison Gallery of Art, at Andover, Massachusetts, is so installed as to show the detachment. This one of oak and the pine figurehead from the *White Lady* from New Bedford seem to be by the same carver. The forward lean distinguishes the figurehead from the more static poses of other wood statues.

Some attractive figureheads are extremely simple, like the

FIG. 2. *Figurehead, three-quarter-length, from the Julia Lawrence.*

old-time Sailor.[24] He is carved out of a single section of a pine tree trunk, sixty-nine inches high. The tree was cut on a slant top and bottom; thereby the figure is given its forward lean. The Sailor has the characteristic raised chin and eyes fixed on the distance. The base on which he stands shows some slight carved decoration; except for this the figure is plain. Before this Sailor came into a private collection, he was found in Norfolk, Virginia, coming probably from a ship that was broken up in the local shipyards.

The bust of a Naval Officer (Plate I) also has the typical forward lean. The shoulders are really narrow; it is not just the effect of the three-quarter view. The craftsman felt no need to follow the natural proportions; the academic artist would have solved his problem differently. The carved-leaf scrolls, here used as a base and for a transition, show how a traditional motif from style art is taken over in folk art. The bold cutting and broad surfaces are in marked contrast to the finished marbles of the academic sculptor. Sharp edges and irregular contours are more characteristic of wood carving than are rounded forms and smooth finish.

Costume played a part in figurehead carving and is well illustrated in the *Belle of Bath*.[25] She was built in Bath, Maine, in 1877 and Charles A. L. Sampson (D. 1881) carved her figurehead with the assistance of Edbury Hatch. Her modish Victorian costume is said to have been the sensation of the day. When the ship stopped at Bangor on her transatlantic voyage, the inhabitants came out for the occasion and admired the figurehead. It shows a costume that was virtually a fashionplate, something of a novelty in figurehead carving. Here no breeze blows; the brand-new gown is shown with the folds unruffled, arranged as it came from the dressmaker's. Carvers were not bound by tradition; they could be up-to-date (Plate II), in a dress that is in the style but without elaborate effects of drapery that would have increased costs. It is an unassuming piece of work, of the same type as the *Samuel Skolfield*. It is noteworthy that figurehead carvers were willing to deal with contemporary costume, and that they did so successfully.

If a ship's name was Barbara, Nancy or Sally, a wife or daughter of the owner may have furnished the inspiration, and such a figurehead might be represented in contemporary costume. In that case, the hairdress, too, would be contemporary, in some such fashion as we see illustrated in *Sartain's Magazine*. Around the mid-nineteenth century a lady busthead (Fig. 3) might show smooth hair parted in the middle and descending on each side in a curve, with pinned-up braids in back.[26]

FIG. 3. *Figurehead, half-length, nineteenth century.*

In female figureheads of the three-quarter-length type, drapery, gathered in bunchy knots, is used conveniently to form a transition to the scroll base.[27] In the half-length figurehead, the Victorian dress could be fitted to the top of a scroll without the necessity of a transition. This is the case with a figurehead taken from the whaler *Marcia*, dated about 1832.[28] Feminine curves and leaf-and-scroll curves go well together; the figurehead designer should have been relieved every time a female was chosen as the figurehead.

A half-length male figurehead in modern costume required a more drastic solution on the part of the designer. The stovepipe-like masculine trousers made for difficulties, but were hard to avoid.

At times the ship's owner is represented, as in the *Samuel Skolfield* (Fig. 4), wearing a frock coat and holding a roll of ship's plans. Note his broad chest, his cylindrical neck, his bulging chin and rounded head, that combine to make him look

FIG. 4. *Figurehead from the* Samuel Skolfield II, *from Portland, Maine, 1883.*

so massive. This kind of simplification is often present in folk art, and we need not think of it as cubism, with which it has nothing to do.

In the half-length male figure of *Brooks Walker*[29] in the Mariners' Museum, Newport News, Virginia, the designer also used a drapery motif. A broad cloth draped like a shawl around masculine hips beneath a Prince Albert seems ludicrous, as fashions go, but is not unreasonable from a point of view of abstract design. In this case, the individualized features and the full beard clearly suggest the portrait, already indicated by the name.

The construction of the figurehead usually took several blocks of wood doweled together; arms were made separately and attached. To avoid splintering, the carving was with the grain of the wood, and details had to be adjusted to the grain. A section of tree trunk might suffice for the torso, but a carver would have had to search the forests to find a tree with a limb so placed as to serve for an outstretched arm. It was more practical to carve the arm separately. In order that the figurehead might not be damaged during a storm, an outstretched arm was sometimes made detachable; it could be removed after the vessel had left port and replaced before she entered the next harbor, when she was expected to look her best.[30] When the old sailing vessels were broken up and the materials sold off, parts of figureheads were lost. That may be why this half-length figurehead is without arms.

In one case an arm was attached by a V-shaped projection on the arm fitted into a V-shaped slot on the bust, allowing the arm to be both secure and demountable. This method is illustrated on a figurehead in the Mariners' Museum, Newport News, Virginia, said to be from the *Black Prince*,[31] perhaps a ship of that name that was built in Newburyport, Massachusetts, in 1857. The leaf-and-scroll decorations that formed a base-like termination of a busthead may be carved on two adjoining blocks. In one three-quarter-length male figure, the costume is sliced off at the shoulders where the now missing arms were attached. His left hand, resting on his hip, is carved out of the main block and still shows as an isolated, cut-off hand.[32]

The simplest type had no arms at all, but only head, neck and chest, with a scroll replacing the arms on each side. This may be seen in an example at the Old Dartmouth Historical Society,[33] the Whaling Museum of New Bedford, Massachusetts.

Bustheads grow out of a scroll or leaf carving, or rest on top, as on a shelf. Carved drapery makes a transition between bust and scroll.[34] Often there is no transition, the drapery is a way of giving a finish to arms below the shoulder. The folk carver seems to have worried more about these cut-off arms; the academic sculptor simply refrained from calling attention to any lack of arms.

Smaller vessels, like whalers, had only an eagle (Fig. 5) as a bow decoration. It is surprising how much variety is possible in even so simple a motif as an eagle. Only the head is shown, and the carving terminates where the neck begins with a scroll or leaf design finishing off the decoration.

Fig. 5. *Eagle, part of a figurehead of the* Great Republic, *1853, perhaps by S. W. or William B. Gleason of Boston.*

If we compare these carved eagle heads, we find that about the only thing they have in common is that all six look like eagles. The beaks differ in length and shape, the eyes are individual, no two being alike; the setting of. the eye varies, and finally the feathers show a variety of techniques.[35]

Pilothouse eagles[36] belong to steamers; they appeared when figureheads on sailing vessels were on the way out. Pilothouse eagles were carved in the round, gilt, and attached at the base. They stand with lifted wings on a globe or rope base. One[37] at the Mariners' Museum is about two and a half feet high. The wings are carved separately and are made to slip into grooves. Another,[38] about three feet high, was carved in New York for use on a Great Lakes steamer. It was washed ashore in 1908 after a storm in which two ships were wrecked. Another pilothouse eagle[39] at the Davenport, Iowa, Public Museum was carved in the shipyards of Cincinnati, Ohio, by Best and Company, in 1845 for service on a Mississippi River boat. The eagle has a wingspread of four and a half feet and is carved of solid oak, in a broad style with a disproportionately large head and a sturdy neck.

Historic ornament, used sparingly by American carvers, survived in the billethead.

A billethead (Fig. 6) consists of a voluted scroll, elaborated more or less with carved leaves and minor scroll work, gilt or painted. This type of decoration formed a part of the traditional architectural heritage of the Classic and Baroque periods. Billetheads that have survived are carved usually with such competence as to suggest that scroll and leaf belonged to the basic vocabulary of the craft. They are closer to academic art than is the case with many sternboards.[40] The best ones may be early or on occasion may be from foreign ships.

Figureheads, being mostly human in form, attract our attention; we are apt to forget that a ship also has a stern. Sternboards were carved mostly in low relief, except for a central motif like a bust, which may be in high relief. Those sternboards that have survived represent truly the tail-end of a glorious past. As those in command of the ship at sea increased their influence over ship design, a more functional type of stern de-

FIG. 6. *Billethead from the ship* Favorite, *nineteenth century*.

veloped. The sternboard carried the ship's name, a portrait or a pictorial representation of the owner, or an eagle, usually with a shield containing the stars and stripes. In the sternpiece of the *John Penrose* (FIG. 26), of the early part of the nineteenth century, the portrait of the owner is placed between two leaf ornaments, carved in a simplified folk-art manner. The way a scarf is wrapped around the shoulders without transition may seem awkward; an academic designer might have finished off the bust in a more elegant fashion. But the folk designer is consistent; he solves his problems in a forthright manner; the same scale is felt throughout and the scarf fits the space.

Eagle-carved sternboards were popular from 1850 to 1880. Some are from five to six feet wide; others may be thirteen feet and wider.[41] Designs are mostly of the spread-eagle type, as the horizontal extension fitted the shape of the stern. The eagle holds a shield showing stars and stripes, but the stars were used as ornament and their number suggests no relation to the number of states in the Union. Crossed flags,[42] sunbursts[43] and band-

FIG. 7. *Inn sign, from New Hampshire.*

eroles with *E Pluribus Unum*[44] are also used. As in the Great Seal, the eagle grasps arrows and olive branch, or he may be perched on rocks or on a globe. The eagles are gilt and the shield is painted in the national colors; there is no single preferred design. The outstretched wings may arch up or down; the head may be pointing in one of various directions. Carvers showed a good deal of independence in the postures they invented to create designs to their liking. The American eagle is a lively bird, and noisy, and is often represented with open beak as if screeching, or lunging forward with outstretched neck. In some instances realism went so far as to show the eagle with one wing foreshortened, creating an unfortunate effect of distortion, ill-suited to the basic problem of decorating a space.[45] In some cases the eagle is but the central motif of a scroll-carved sternboard painted black with the decorations in gilt.[46]

PLATE II. *Tea-store Figure, nineteenth century.*

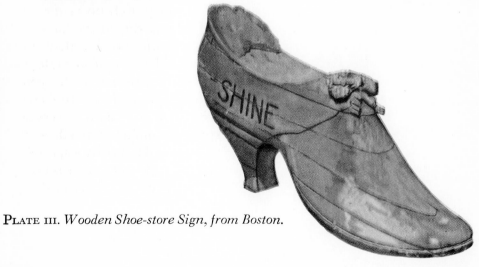

PLATE III. *Wooden Shoe-store Sign, from Boston.*

Occasionally the history of a ship carving is known. A sailing vessel, the *Columbia*, had an eagle-carved sternboard over twenty feet wide (Fig. 8),[47] known to have been carved around 1870 by a certain J. Nabor. In 1877 the vessel was wrecked in a hurricane, but the sternboard was picked up and came into the possession of the widow of the carver, who presented it to the Louisiana State Museum.

To a smaller group of ship carvings belong mast sheaths[48] and gangboards. An elaborately carved mast sheath is owned by the Old Dartmouth Whaling Museum at New Bedford. The design of leaves, cornucopias and ornamental borders is unique in its freedom and vigor. Gangboards carved with eagles have also been preserved, as in the Chicago Historical Society,[49] the Portsmouth, New Hampshire, Historical Society, and elsewhere.

Fig. 8. *Sternpiece from the ship* Columbia, *by J. Nabor, 1870.*

The carving of figureheads was a craft that was based on the apprenticeship system of master, journeyman and apprentice.[50] Foremost among master carvers were William Rush of Philadelphia, John and Simeon Skillin of Boston and Samuel McIntire of Salem. Apprentices trained in their shops carried on the craft into the nineteenth century. Shop-trained carvers developed a style of carving that was used on land and sea. For instance the figurehead carver, Edward S. Griffin of Portland, Maine, around 1850 also carved doors and mantels and was interested in painting and sculpture. He was versatile and a man of broad sympathies in the arts, and yet we should call the figureheads he carved folk art.

In the early eighties commissions for figureheads had become so scarce that most of the few carvers still in business worked on fancy carving and scroll work for yachts. This was a type of work that was "too accurate and artistic to suit the sailor, who liked to see things rough-hewn."[51]

A well-known name in ship carving of the late nineteenth century is that of John Haley Bellamy (1836–1914). He had a shop in Kittery, Maine, across the river from Portsmouth, New Hampshire, and he did much of his work for the Navy, but also worked for commercial shipbuilders. One of his best-known works is the great eagle he carved for the U.S.S. *Lancaster*.[52] The eagle, which had a wingspread of eighteen feet, is now on exhibition in the Marine Museum of Portsmouth, Virginia. Bellamy is known for small spread eagles, carved of pine, painted white and touched up with the red and blue of the American flag, or with a star. He made them in quantities and gave many away to friends. The templates he used and his shop drawings have been preserved by Joseph W. P. Frost, a descendant. Bellamy was a student of literature who wrote for Maine and New Hampshire newspapers.[53] He is known to have attended some art school, but the name of the school is not remembered.

The names and addresses of hundreds of ship carvers are known from city directories, newspapers and other records.[54] Most of them lived on the eastern seaboard. From the point of view of identification, the surviving figureheads fall into four groups. In one small group[55] we know the names of carvers and figureheads. In a second,[56] we know the subject of the figure-head, but not carver or ship. For those of a third group,[57] we know the name of the ship for which it was carved; for a fourth group, information is entirely lacking. Pauline Pinckney[58] has published a list of over 700 wood carvers, which includes ship carvers.

# CHAPTER II

# SHOP FIGURES AND
# AMUSEMENT PROPS

Wood-carved shop figures and tavern signs have been in use in this country for well over two hundred years. The use of the human figure in shop signs, common in the eighteenth century, gradually went out of fashion, but carved boots (Plate III), gloves, clocks, spectacles, razors, mortars and the like continued almost into our own period. The barber pole is the only one that is still with us, though it is no longer carved of wood. There are two types of carved shop figure: the older, traditional, eighteenth-century type, produced by professional artisans, and a later, nineteenth-century cigar-store Indian. The best remembered and most widely used in its day was the cigar-store figure, which achieved a truly native American expression. We shall begin with the older, traditional type.

This gentleman (Fig. 9), with 1720 on his belt, was carved fully a century before wooden Indians became common. The costume, with blue coat over red vest, knee breeches and buckled shoes, may be that of a civilian rather than a soldier. His right hand is thrust into his vest; his left may have held the hilt of a sword. His head is turned slightly to one side, and there is a jovial expression on his face. This man is striking a pose; he appears confident and was meant to look friendly, to attract business to shop or tavern.

The man who made this figure was a professional craftsman, better trained than most later shop-figure carvers. The necessity of getting the posture out of a block of wood limited the amount of action that was possible, even where arms were at-

FIG. 9. *Inn sign or shop figure.*

tached separately. In spite of block restrictions, an easy pose is effected in the difference of the slope of the shoulders, and in the left arm that is well separated from the body. This figure follows a tradition in the manner of an established craft. It has a consistency of style that is pleasing. Note the heavy manner throughout, in the fully rounded hands, arms and legs; the massive head and the full cheeks. Even the coat tails and pockets have the thickness that is needed in wood to keep edges from breaking off.

Several other eighteenth-century shop figures[1] are known. One is the so-called Little Admiral with 1770 on the base. It served as a sign for William Williams, a mathematical instrument maker at No. 1 Long Wharf, Boston, and is now in the Old State House. The carving is bulky and the pose is free, in the manner of the other eighteenth-century shop figures. Action is suggested in a doll-like manner, except that dolls often have movable limbs; here they are doweled in, and legs and feet are well separated. Such shop figures retain a basic gawkiness; they stand stiff because the wooden block out of which the trunk is carved is essentially vertical, and they are under life size. This figure and the tailor's shop sign are of the same style and period.

Other shop figures in the same tradition include a coachman, wearing a three-cornered hat, a blue coat, yellow waistcoat and breeches, and high black boots, and a tobacconist's figure of 1770 in Demuth's Tobacco Shop in Lancaster, Pennsylvania.

In 1776 four British prisoners of war found themselves together in one jail in Windham, Connecticut. They were fed by the innkeeper, Widow Cary, whom they presented upon their release with a carved figure of Bacchus[2] (Plate IV). One of them, John Russell, was a ship's carpenter. With his three cell mates he carved the plump infant Bacchus seated astride a keg and holding before him a basket filled with fruit. The back of his head is overlaid with grapes and leaves; the figure is painted flesh color; the barrel is red with black hoops and the date 1776 is carved across the front of the keg. The figure is about twenty-six inches high; the keg twenty-one inches long. Here we have a sample of eighteenth-century English folk carving executed with gusto and good humor. According to tradition, the prisoners were only allowed the use of a pocket knife. The Windham Bacchus, a landmark, is now kept at the Library.

Two busts,[3] man and woman, perhaps tavern figures, are comparable in spirit to the Windham Bacchus, and equal in merit. They are alike in style; apparently they were carved by the same hand and were probably used together. Such lively expression with broad grins and hunched shoulders is also the work of professional carvers; probably English, perhaps at the time of the Revolution. Though European in style, they could have been carved in this country.

The eighteenth-century tradition is further illustrated by two ships' chandlers' figures; one,[4] at the New York State Historical Association at Cooperstown, New York; and another[5] (Plate V) in the King Philip Museum at Mount Hope, Rhode Island. The former may reflect an English tradition. Arms and legs, awkward though they may be, are nevertheless free of the torso. This tradition continued into the nineteenth century, and is illustrated in another nautical instrument-maker's shop figure of a naval officer[6] from Philadelphia, holding up a sextant to make an observation. Other examples of this free pose tradition include a figure of a Highlander[7] made by William Allen (1824), a Scotsman[8] in kilts and holding a pinch of snuff, and a Negro,[9] representing Headache, with freely disposed limbs, a figure said to have been used in the show of a traveling medicine man.

This older tradition of small, under-life-size figures, is basically different from the typical nineteenth-century, practically life-size cigar-store Indian. Occasionally the traditions may have merged, but nineteenth-century tobacconists' figure carving drew to itself less experienced carvers. They were probably aided by ship carvers, as ship carving was declining. Such a view is supported by certain resemblances between figurehead and cigar-store-Indian carving. In both, one arm is carved out of the tree trunk, and often both arms. The cigar-store figures themselves include a new, more primitive type of carving that appeared with the expanding cigar-store business.

Shops other than those of the tobacconists had their individual emblems and these shops adhered to a more traditional style. Instrument makers had a midshipman or naval officer, with sextant or spyglass. Drug stores varied in emblems used. Emerson's drug store in Salem, Massachusetts, had a wood-carved bust of Paracelsus,[10] the renowned German-Swiss physician of the sixteenth century. The bust, dating from about 1840, is now in the Essex Institute.[11] The carver must have been a sculptor trained in the classicizing style of the period. It was once painted white in imitation of marble, and suggests an influence from the idealizing busts of Hellenistic antiquity, perhaps infused with another element that was meant to come closer to something Germanic.

The Llado Drug Store in New Orleans, Louisiana, in the mid-nineteenth century had at Chartres and Dumaine Streets a wood-carved figure (Plate VI) about five and a half feet high: a Negro, wearing a tin cap and holding a big wooden pestle in a tin mortar.. The carving is skillful, realistic, probably of local origin, and different from the tobacconists' type.[12] A third wood-carved version of an apothecary's sign[13] is Colonel Sellers (Plate VII), a figure four and a half feet high. It represents a promoter of patent medicine, a character from *The Gilded Age* by Mark Twain and Charles Dudley Warner.

These shop figures and tavern signs were placed outside. There was another smaller type of advertising figure attached to a base that stood inside the shop. Those that have survived appear in uniform or in civilian clothes, and were probably used by tailors who specialized in uniform or in civilian dress.

To this group belong figures in uniform, about twenty-six inches high, carved out of a single block and painted over a gesso base, with detachable head, as a Civil War General from Freehold, New Jersey.

A tailor's shop sign (Fig. 10) from Pennsylvania is of the nineteenth century. It is about twenty-six inches tall. It probably came from a country store, where it was used as a counter figure. Its style shows no resemblance to the earlier professional shop figure but the type existed, as we know from an example fourteen inches high showing George Washington in an eighteenth-century costume. The carver was an amateur, hence the small feet and tiny, claw-like hands, the big head and staring eyes. After the carver had exhausted his efforts on achieving a likeness to George Washington, he found there were not enough inches left for the rest of the figure. The head is ghastly serious and exerts a strange fascination. It gives the impression of being free-floating, suspended without support and without substance except for the painful exactitude of the clothes. A companion figure from the same region represented Thomas Jefferson.

These earlier shop figures disappeared before the time of the older generation of today, but many of us still have vivid recollections of the wooden Indians on the sidewalks in front of cigar stores. A wooden Indian stood before virtually every tobacco shop during the period of their heyday, from the late fifties to the eighties of the nineteenth century. The Indian (Plate VIII) identified the tobacco store as readily as the red-and-white-striped pole marks the barber shop. The number of such figures in actual use today is small. As late as 1937, a count [14] of cigar-store figures listed 585 in forty-two states. Many are in the possession of dealers and collectors; a few are in historical museums and practically none in art museums. As folk art, they

Fig. 10. *Tailor's shop figure, from Pennsylvania.*

have received no attention from art museums. Garish color may have hindered appreciation of the shop figure as an art form. Exposed to the weather, they had to be kept bright and shiny. The effect of periodical repainting is repellent to tastes accustomed to a natural patina which is acquired with time. The calculated effect of the grain of the wood as used by modern sculptors is also absent. A shop figure was the storekeeper's advertisement, not an investment in art. If the Indian attracted attention and increased business, he had fulfilled his duty.

A smaller variant of the life-sized American figure was known in England[15] as early as the seventeenth century. These English "Black Boys" or "Virginians" are little grotesque figures, not over thirty inches high, and unlike the American Indian type. They lack the monumental character of our wooden Indians, and had no influence on American cigar-store Indians.

During the eighteenth century, tobacconists' figures were still uncommon in this country. A figure of Pocahontas is said to have existed in Boston[16] on Hancock Street in 1730; and in Lancaster,[17] Pennsylvania, as early as 1770 the aforementioned gentleman extending a snuffbox stood outside the tobacco shop of Christopher Demuth. Baltimore[18] has also been credited with cigar-store Indians before 1780, but the carving of these figures as a business belongs to the nineteenth century.

As mentioned before, cigar-store Indians were at times made by the same men who carved figureheads.[19] The man who introduced carved figures as tobacco signs in New York, according to Weitenkampf, was Chicester, carver between 1850 and 1860. Eventually, as the ship carvings declined, the wooden Indians took over.[20] Thomas W. Brooks, who was a ship carver in New York for at least thirty-five years, also carved and sold Indians, according to his son. Sculptors in the academic tradition occasionally carved cigar-store Indians, Julius Theodore Melchers of Detroit and Herman Matzen of Cleveland being among them.[21]

Shop figures were sold from New York, Chicago, Philadelphia, Baltimore and Detroit to tobacco shops all over the country.[22] One salesman is said to have worked with illustrated catalogs, descriptions, prices and the latest discounts on thirty chiefs and "extra special Pocahontases."[23]

It is said that of the figures made in New York in 1890, nearly all came from the shop of S. A. Robb, who had been in business for nearly twenty-six years.[24] However, according to another report, in 1887 six firms were still in business, employing from twenty to thirty carvers, who produced from two to three hundred wooden Indians each year.[25] It seems that by then the business was declining; the demand had probably been met. There was a limit to the number of tobacco shops and the figures were remarkably long-lived. The business of rejuvenating cigar-store figures eventually became as brisk as the production of new ones.[26] Full-sized new Indians sold for from fifty to one hundred dollars; those carved by Melchers brought more, from one hundred fifty up. Second-hand figures that had been traded in for new ones, when repaired and repainted, were resold.[27]

The designs fall into four groups: Chiefs, Squaws or Pocahontases, Blackamoors or Pompeys, and White Men.[28] This last class included Sir Walter Raleighs, Uncle Sams, Lord Dundrearys, Forty-niners, policemen, Punches, Highlanders, the Chinese figure (Plate II) of the tea stores, and others. The Indians proper were subdivided; an Indian with his hand shading his eyes was called a "scout"; holding a gun or bow and arrow he was a "hunting chief," and if he had his head shaved except for the scalplock he was a "Captain Jack."

Frank Weitenkampf[29] as a young reporter in 1890 secured some first-hand information on the carving of wooden Indians in New York City. He mentions that logs of white pine were secured from the local spar yards; this suggests that perhaps carvers as well as logs came from the water front. Regarding the actual carving, the report is not quite clear. He mentions the use of paper patterns, and states that the log, during the carving, was so disposed that it "hung freely." It is to be hoped that further research will throw additional light on the method of carving the figures.

After the main proportions were roughed out, the figure was finished with the chisel and finally painted. Arms and hands might be made separately and screwed on. If the figure was cut in one piece, the arms were held close to the body, giving a solid and chunky effect.

As is the case with figureheads, some of the best carvings are the simplest. In this under-life-sized cigar-store Indian (Fig. 11) we have the basic posture, one arm raised and bent, the other stretched, both clinging to the figure. There is no influence from academic art, but only the craft tradition of the ship carver. The block has been cut into as little as possible; we are aware of the original block which still shows at the base and at the back. Just enough wood has been removed to reveal massive proportions and broad surfaces throughout. The figure is like a bundle with some indentations. Details, a feather headdress and tobacco leaves, are all but suppressed; the total mass seems to draw to itself everything that might protrude beyond the contour. Form is in one compact mass; the outstretched arm melts

Fig. 11. *Cigar-store figure, from Maryland, under life size.*

unobtrusively into the figure. Even the raised and bent arm is but a lump, only slightly differentiated from chest and shoulder. The knee of the right leg stands out and was no doubt close to the surface of the original log. The volume is expanded so much that we no longer feel that a standard pose was forced upon the carver; he was able to accommodate his style to the limiting block.

There is hardly an indication of drapery; a few cuts across the grain suggest folds. Wood carving requires that the carver cut away the material, instead of adding it, as in clay modeling; he is constantly aware of the danger of cutting too deep and taking away too much. This trains him to preserve the large surface and retain the simple geometric shapes; he works for design rather than for realism. Although this basic pose is not an unusual one in cigar-store Indians, the upturned head makes this figure unique. The carver may have worked on figureheads before he turned to shop figures, and for that reason had not quite overcome the habit of the raised head and the gaze fixed on the distance. This figure was once owned in Baltimore, and could have been made there.

This Indian Squaw (Fig. 13) may remind us of Egyptian art. It follows the law of frontality; one foot is placed before the other; one arm is raised and the other held close to the body. But this is not a copy of an Egyptian statue. It is only superficially like an Egyptian figure. Egyptian sculpture has more rigidity, greater refinement, more delicacy and nothing of the relaxation, which is clearly an expression of nineteenth-century realism. The carver decided on the pose because it seemed appropriate and within the range of his skill.

A Pocahontas often held a rose instead of a tomahawk, and had more attractive features. Otherwise, squaws looked pretty much like braves, in costume and in the proportions of the figure.

The Chief holding out a package of cigars shows the same type in freer action. The carver, struggling to give his figure some feeling of life, suggests action by freeing the arm. In another version, the figure may hold a leaf of tobacco, a tomahawk, knife or rifle, or raise an arm in friendly salute after the

FIG. 12. *Cigar-store figure.*

Indian custom. The cigar-store figures were not meant to be authentic Indians,[30] either in costume or in emblems. They are advertising dummies, showing at best a general resemblance to Indians. The types repeat, but there are minor variations in carving. To an extent, variations came about through copying by different carvers, for there was no way to make exact duplicates by a mechanical device. As a rule, a new figure is an adaptation of an old one.

Ordinarily, carvers remained low-paid artisans, some more skillful than others; a few had received professional training.[31] S. A. Robb is said to have studied at the New York Academy of

Design. The figures carved by sculptors are easily recognized, occasionally showing the influence of classic art. In one example[32] (Fig. 12), the pose is based on the well-known ancient Roman statue of Emperor Augustus addressing his army.[33] The

FIG. 13. *Cigar-store Indian, Pocahontas.*

greater freedom in pose and the more accomplished technique set such figures apart from the common type. Occasionally, where academically trained carvers were at work, preliminary drawings may have been used, but hardly otherwise.

Illustrations, prints or real Indians do not appear to have been of any influence on shop figures, and it was the exception for the carver to rely on models. A reporter who interviewed a manufacturer of wooden Indians was told: "Fidelity to nature or artistic beauty is not much looked for. That Indian," and the speaker pointed to a melancholy flat-nosed chief, "was done from life and we can't sell him. Buyers complain that he is too ugly. What they want is something fine-looking and attractive."[34]

There is a tradition associated with a certain wooden Indian (Fig. 14), Big Chief Me-Smoke-Em,[35] for which an Iroquois chief served as a model. This later Indian now looks straight ahead, no longer up. The figure from the head down shows the conventional pose, varied only in costume details. The type exists in several versions. In one, the Indian holds in his left hand a rifle that was said to have been used against the Indians in the massacre of Fort Dearborn; in another he holds a tomahawk. In both versions the right hand offers a package of cigars. One Indian of this type belonged to a Chicago shop and survived the Chicago fire. According to the story, Indians making purchases in this shop would recognize the chief, and would give some guttural indication that they well knew who was represented. Head and features are realistic. Otherwise the figure remains primitive in anatomical details, but the decorations are elaborate and the appearance is impressive. In this case a skilled craftsman did the head, after which the carving could have been turned over to assistants to complete the figure, carving the arms separately and attaching them.

As cigar-store Indians were made in quantities to sell at a price, the owner of the business could hardly be expected to turn out individualized sculpture.

In another case, Sitting Bull is said to have served as the model for a cigar-store Indian carved in 1842 by Herman Kruske for Bob Parson's tobacco shop in Ashland, Wisconsin.[36]

PLATE IV. *Bacchus, by John Russell and assistants at Windham, Connecticut, 1776.*

FIG. 14. *Cigar-store Indian, c. 1865. Iroquois Chief, used in Chicago, Illinois.*

Cigar-store Indians may also be divided into groups from the point of view of posture. Usually, the simpler the pose, the less experienced the carver, and the more primitive the figure will appear. Occasionally an experienced carver may choose a simple posture. It is also true that a carver of limited skill may adhere to a simple pose and still achieve a pleasing effect. An arrangement progressing from immobility to freedom is therefore not necessarily one of increased artistic merit.

The types are as follows:

(1) A flat profile figure.[37] It is sawed out of a thick board, which was fastened to a baseboard by means of angle-irons for a solid support. There were probably few of this flat type, as they were not sufficiently impressive to be sold to a dealer. In its simplest form, the type shows no work of the chisel; the sharp saw-cut contour is allowed to remain. The type is obviously a home-made substitute, used perhaps locally where a more professional figure was not available. But this type also occurs with the edges rounded off and with some slight variation in the thickness of the figure. Most cigar-store figures are carved in the round.

(2) The basic type[38] has one arm pressed to his side, the other bent and held in front. Both feet are flat on the ground, often one in front of the other. Variations[39] show both arms, bent or extended, or concealed by a shawl or blanket, except for the hands. One arm may even be separated from the body to leave a small opening between elbow and hip.

(3) Both arms are bent, and one or both extended forward, free of the body.[40]

(4) One arm is raised, holding cigars or a tomahawk.[41]

(5) One or both arms are in part detached from the body.[42]

(6) The right arm is raised to the forehead in Indian salute.[43]

These typical poses occur in males and females, or chiefs and Pocahontases, as they are called. Similarities are more apparent than differences.

Though many cigar-store Indians have been destroyed, there

is so much repetition among them that remaining types are probably sufficient for an over-all impression of the total production. A grouping of cigar-store Indians according to posture brings into focus this element of set convention. Repetition of motifs within a limited range is a characteristic of folk art. If we refrain from limiting the designation, folk art, to European peasant art, most cigar-store Indians are folk art.

Carvers were largely artisans who followed a routine which permitted a degree of freedom in details. It remains to be investigated to what extent minor variations can be used to define the manner of one shop or one individual against the manner of another shop or a different individual.

A smaller number of cigar-store figures show no standardized poses but some freedom of action. Capable artisans or even experienced sculptors were at times attracted to the carving of the Indians. This gives us

(7) A group closer to the academic level. The figures of this small group at times show an influence from classical sculpture. This is true of a figure[44] in which the pose is that of the aforementioned Roman statue of Emperor Augustus addressing his army. This figure, a Pocahontas (Fig. 13) is freely composed, showing a lively gait with no resemblance to the usual awkward postures of a more typical figure. Cigars, a tobacco leaf belt and a feather headdress have been retained, but the costume has been simplified and the color has faded to a harmonious blend of neutral tints. In another figure,[45] closely related, the posture and details show minor variations.

There are other figures that show more than the usual action and greater individuality, though no obvious reliance on classical sculpture. They may have grown out of the accumulated experience. One such figure, a Pocahontas,[46] is in the Pony Express Museum of Arcadia, California. The owner, dating it about 1846, stated that it came to the west coast from Philadelphia. Another Pocahontas[47] is thought to date from about 1870; it is unusual in the slender proportions and the freedom of action, with the left arm swung free from the body in an obvious trial for grace. A chief[48] shows a lively action, but one that might well represent a unique achievement of what could be called the native, unacademic tradition. The motion of legs and arms is in one forward direction, with no side movement. For vigor and conviction, this figure is exceptional. A tobacconist's figure in the Maryland Historical Society, Baltimore, is closer to some classic type. Conceived as a Mercury,[49] this figure has bare muscular legs, a helmet and is clothed in a short coat with breast armor and leather lappets in the fashion of a Roman soldier.

An example of the "white type" of shop figure is represented in the *Victorian Lady* (Fig. 15). The fact that she reveals her ankles shows how daring the tobacconists had become, and the lengths to which they would go to attract customers. A young lady who sold cigars in the days of our grandparents would be expected to make concessions to the mannish business in which she was engaged. That may be why her costume shows a touch of the fashionable riding habit, a permissible departure from strict femininity. It also may be significant that this figure comes from Arizona, a western state where women were in the minority and where any woman, even a wooden one, would attract attention.

The dress with its ruffles is elaborate, but the carver simplified his design. Wherever there are three or four folds close together, they are alike in width, thickness and direction. One may speak of this type of figure carving as realistic, but the realism is in the general effect; it is based on ornamental pattern.

Isaac Fowle, figurehead carver of Boston, made a sign (Mass. Ca. 25) for the hardware dealer John Bradford, at 13 Dock Square. With a semicircular space at his disposal, he filled it with saws and planes and other carpentry tools in the manner of a relief. He carved the sign out of a single panel and went at his task as an architect might have done. Instead of hanging out a saw in the way a shoemaker hangs out his shoe, he arranged tools into an architectural setting, in place of scroll and acanthus leaves. Here is one of those early American attempts to solve problems in a forthright manner. It is a parallel on the folk-art level to Latrobe's desire for originality in his corncob capitals in the Corn Foyer of the Capitol building in Washington.

FIG. 15. *Cigar-store figure.*

An attractive aspect of early carved shop signs is an occasional instance of sly humor, or at least a note of piquancy. There is something provocative in the combination of a huge butcher knife used as a support for a man driving a pig (Plate X). The happy-go-lucky unconcern of this butcher's sign sticks in one's mind; it must have been good advertising. The original of 1835 from Fairhaven, Massachusetts, is now in the New Bedford Whaling Museum.

A much-admired relief-carved sheaf of wheat (Fig. 16) was made by Clarke Noble around 1900 for a bakery building. Heads and stems are individually carved in detail, and yet the

FIG. 16. *Shop sign, Sheaf of Wheat, carved by Clarke Noble.*

total effect is restful. The simplicity of the contour of the sheaf contributes to a most decorative effect. The original is at the Newport, Rhode Island, Historical Society.

Wood continued to be used for the three-dimensional shop signs, as in the carved horses' heads over livery stables.[50]

Though the modern circus goes back to the early nineteenth century, the circus carvings that have survived are of the 1880's, 1890's and later. The trap wagons which carried the equipment had to be disguised, so the wagon builders employed wood carvers, who decorated the exteriors with carved figures[51] and scroll work, painted and gilded.

For the carvers, it was a job to be turned out on contract as part of a day's work. Today we look upon these battered figures with fresh eyes and discover a fascination of which their own period was unaware. Unfortunately, not much is left; circus carvings perished before anyone thought them worth preserving, and even the drawings for wagons and carvings have been destroyed.

One of these circus figures (Fig. 17) was inspired by the well-known "Wounded Amazon" type of Greek sculpture. As a part of the total decoration of a circus wagon, painted white and gilt, a figure was intended only for a fleeting glance. That explains the awkward poses and the hurried execution. Though circus figures were not taken seriously, even in their own day, details are often surprisingly fine, as in this head, which suggests archaic sculpture. If we look at circus carvings with unprejudiced eyes, we find they are not all alike.

Another figure[52] with a magnificent head shows a fine stateliness. It may perhaps be a reflection of some classic statue, several times removed.

Another, a Muse with Lyre,[53] of about 1880, was one of several figures applied to the side of a wagon owned by Barnum and Bailey. The carver combined motifs of classical drapery for the sake of a decorative effect. Drapery and figure exist side by side almost independent of each other. This approaches a free mingling of shapes where forms glide past each other to start movements of their own. A complete disintegration of visual appearance, here suggested, became a principle in modern art and finally ended in pure abstraction. Samuel Robb, who worked for the Sebastian Wagon Company of New York who built the wagons, may have carved this figure.

FIG. 17. *Circus wagon figure for Bar-num and Bailey. Carved by Samuel Robb.*

A Jenny Lind[54] was carved about 1875, a quarter century after the famous Swedish Nightingale made her first appearance in New York. The carver simplified his forms and shapes and gave her a costume she probably would never have worn. The carving in broad simplified masses is in the manner of the folk artist.

A number of circus wagons had been stored by a circus company on a farm outside the city of Bridgeport, Connecticut. For some years the circus company paid for storage, but eventually payments fell behind, while the wagons, exposed to the weather, deteriorated year by year. The gold leaf disappeared, scraped off by neighbor boys who are said to have sold it. The owner, finally wishing to clear his property of the ruins, burned the wagons, but first removed the carvings to what has been described as an abandoned still, and advertised them for sale. His ad was in the paper a month without attracting any attention, until it was seen by Mr. William Warren of Litchfield, Connecticut, who acquired the lot. This was the beginning of their rise to prestige. Thus was saved a significant part of our folk carving.[55]

Circus carving lived in the same environment that produced all major decoration in the late nineteenth and early twentieth centuries; a period of eclecticism. Yet circus carving was unacademic without being folk art; perhaps the term "popular art" describes it.

Carrousels were independent of circuses. The American carrousel with its rotating platform is comparatively modern, as it goes back only to 1879, the year the improved version was made in North Tonawanda, New York.

Carrousel horses reflect something of the spirit of the ornate pageantry of the Renaissance. There is a family resemblance to European types, perhaps with less surface carving than appears on English carrousel horses.[56]

Connecticut, Missouri, Rhode Island, Florida and other states have preserved carrousel carvings which were not necessarily made there. The Parker Carnival Supply Company[57] made carrousel carvings in Abilene, Kansas, around 1890. Names of their carvers are not reported. Other carvings were made in New York, Chicago, Milwaukee and probably elsewhere.

A number of horses and other carrousel animals, dating from 1880 and 1888 have been reported as being the work of Charles Louff.[58] His goat[59] and deer[60] are vigorously conceived, boldly carved animals, individualized in action and elaborated with broad bands of carved and painted trappings. His team of tigers are sufficiently tiger-like for carrousel use without attempting to qualify for a habitat group in a museum of natural history. Anatomical correctness was not intended. Even a rabbit is made interesting; only the dog[61] seems flat, as dogs seem to be less suitable for carrousel purposes.

When carrousel horses are in good repair and well painted, they may be objects of visual enjoyment. Compare any half dozen examples and you become aware of the individuality of the carver. A single carrousel horse suggests a formula, deceiving one into the false conclusion that they are all alike. A closer examination reveals the differences. Some[62] are soft and delicate, as if cast in a mold or drawn out of hardened molasses candy. Others are frankly sawed, chopped and chiseled out of wood. Some are like the white steed of a fairy prince; others like escaped and frightened mares.[63]

As the carrousel horses by Charles Louff are known from a number of examples, his formula can be studied and compared with other works of the same class. Carrousel carvings fit into a pattern, or a collection of mannerisms, which is another way of saying that they have a common style.

Charles Louff represents this style in an extravagant form. Characteristics are: individualized action, elaboration of trappings, and a fusion of realism and abstraction to suggest intense liveliness. One of his horses is particularly magnificent, and illustrates carrousel carving in its most Baroque phase (Fig. 18). Most horses stretch their heads forward; here the head is tossed back and to one side. Most horses suggest speed through outstretched legs with little or no difference between the placement of right and left forelegs or hindlegs; here each leg strikes its own pose. Usually the manes are divided into more or less parallel sections of grooves; here the mane is tossed about in wild curls of irregular shapes. Saddle and blanket have carved borders, and there are additional carved decorations. On another

FIG. 18. *Carrousel horse, carved by Charles Louff of Riverside, Rhode Island.*

Louff horse, a winged head carved in the round projects out from the horse's breast.

This carver belonged to the period of carrousel carving that temporarily experimented with other animals besides horses. A pig (Fig. 19) may also be his, judging from the vigorous modeling, the exuberance and animation he gives to his forms which are still formal and stylized. Though they are realistic, they are still prettified for the purpose of a carnival.

FIG. 19. *Carrousel pig, from Newport, Rhode Island.*

There are also carrousel horses that are too well restored; they glisten in the reflections of metallic luster. Others have stood out in the weather so that they blister and open up at the seams (Fig. 20). Carrousel horses are like overgrown toys, amusing in a mock seriousness. The fact that they look so frozen stiff is one of their peculiar charms. Their unconscious humor may be due to their size; their extravagance is there for all to see.

Carrousels, too, had wood-carved figures which stood in front of the steam organ or calliope.[64] Dancers and musicians were favored, in keeping with the spirit of hilarity that the occasion called for. One such figure (Fig. 21) is holding drumsticks in her outstretched hands.[65] Another (Fig. 22) is a ballet girl[66] posing, one foot resting on a sphere while the other leg is grace-fully swung back. The drummer lady in expression and cos-

FIG. 20. *Carrousel horse head, made by Parker Carnival Supply Company, c. 1890 at Leavenworth, Kansas.*

tume suggests an Italian ancestry; the dancer for contrast is a plumpish blonde with luxuriantly disheveled locks, a Germanic type. Both differ in style from the circus wagon figures. The carvers are unknown, though they belong to the recent past. Such work was taken for granted; it served its purpose in the amusement world and attracted no attention in the art world of its day. Looking at these figures, one gets the impression that they belong to a later phase of the craftsman tradition, well toward the end of the nineteenth century.

Puppets and marionettes[67] are toys handled by adults for the amusement of children. They were used in performances that were popular throughout the nineteenth century. The two differ in that a puppet is worked by the hand and fingers inserted glove-like into the figure; marionettes are worked by strings attached to the figures in several places and manipulated

FIG. 21. *Carrousel calliope figure,*
*Girl with Drumsticks.*

FIG. 22. *Carrousel calliope figure, Dancer on Globe.*

from a position above the stage. The heads of both are carved of wood, and they alone are important from the carving point of view.

Puppetry has a long, old-world tradition in which various countries participated. Characters like Punch and Judy (Plate XI) were formed before they came to this country, though American types, like the famous Indian "Rain-in-the-Face" were incorporated into the American repertory.

An important collection of puppets is the well-known set that was made and used by the members of the Lano family; both hand- and string-operated types are represented. Enrico Lano was engaged in puppetry in Milan during the eighteenth century; his son migrated to America in 1825. An occasional puppet in the family set may go back to the late eighteenth century;[68] the set as a whole was made about 1880.[69]

Which members of the family carved the puppets is not reported. David, born around 1874, was teaching puppetry in Michigan in the late thirties. His younger brother Burt was a carver of circus wagons.[70] David and Goliath and Robinson Crusoe are among the plays presented. These puppets are remarkable in the way each type is caricatured. Facial expression ranges from the sweetness of Sally, the innkeeper's daughter who was said to be "pure as the driven snow," to the sadness of the clown who was robbed of his life's savings. The judge who presides over Punch's trial for his life is truly menacing in his ghostlike pallor, and the Devil himself glows with his red cheeks and green eyes reflecting the tortures of hell. For color is as varied as shape, and both together are used imaginatively with gusto. One looks in wonder at these raucous characters, broadly grinning[71] or open-eyed, teeth showing and chins pushed forward as if prepared for a savage attack. There is variety and contrast in the use of color. Certain tricks of painting are repeated, though with different effects; some of them are circus make-up patterns. Devices like the shoe-button eye are in the tradition of the craft itself. Carving and painting merged to produce an effect of grotesque fantasy well suited to slapstick comedy.

The Lano family was not the only one that worked in this

field. John Diefendorfer[72] was another; he is here represented by a hand puppet, "Pirate," of about 1888–1890. Meader,[73] reported as having been active in San Francisco around 1880, carved a type of wooden puppet with movable mouth.

Making puppets has found its place in school art programs and in therapeutic work of hospitals. Early puppets should be of interest to all who work in puppetry.

PLATE V. *Ship Chandler's Sign, c. 1850.*

PLATE VI.   Drug-store figure,
from New Orleans,
Louisiana, c.1850.

# CHAPTER III

# PORTRAITS AND MONUMENTS

The fashionable portrait was modeled in clay to be cut in marble, but occasionally portraits were carved in wood.

Samuel McIntire of Salem,[1] Massachusetts, was cabinet-maker, carver and architect; one hesitates to call him a folk artist. McIntire is the meticulous craftsman, precise, finished and dry. His well-known bust of John Winthrop,[2] first Governor of Massachusetts Bay (1798) (Fig. 23) is a study in ornamental line.[3] With what care the hair is arranged in thick strands, like skeins of yarn laid out neatly one beside the other! McIntire was a carver of ornament; by training and experience he was ill prepared to interpret character. A decorator is likely to carry over from architecture a tendency to repeat shapes rather than to study anatomy and seek out the variations in the structure of the head. Moreover, in carving Governor Winthrop, McIntire was not confronted by a living person.

The bust was carved after a chalk drawing that represented Winthrop as a young man when he was about to leave England. The first Governor of Massachusetts Bay was a gentle soul, a sincere and able person, but there is no reason to believe that. he was as weak as this portrait would indicate, or as tense as the staring eyes make him appear. The bust, originally painted white, has since taken on a warm cream color.

McIntire's bust of Voltaire was presumably carved after some other bust of Voltaire which the artist had before him while at work. A small porcelain bust[4] has been suggested as the most

FIG. 23. *Governor John Winthrop, bust by Samuel McIntire, Salem, Massachusetts, 1798.*

likely model. Stylistically the Winthrop and Voltaire busts are alike; the differences are those demanded by a different subject and another costume.

McIntire also carved several reliefs now in the Essex Institute, including a medallion[5] of Washington, and a figurehead[6] holding a medallion, in the Peabody Museum in Salem. As the figurehead was handed down in the family of McIntire's granddaughter, it is assumed to be his.

Let us turn for comparison to a folk-art bust, a self-portrait[7] carved in 1833 by P. J. Landry. Though Landry was without training, he probably achieved a reasonable likeness in his self-portrait; attractive design compensates for its lack of anatomical correctness. The son of a French immigrant, Pierre Joseph Landry, Junior (1770–1843), pursued the arts as an avocation. Through illness in old age he was forced into a sedentary life and then returned to his early artistic interests. We get a vivid impression of the old gentleman at work on his self-portrait through the recollections of an old lady of Iberville, Louisiana.[8] In 1913 she still remembered having seen the wood carver, when she was a little girl. She recalled his workbench that stood beside his chair, and the shining knives he used while at work. She also recalled having heard people say that the bust was an excellent likeness, and that "when working on it he surrounded himself with mirrors so that he could catch his reflection from every angle."

There are several other wood carvings, now in the Louisiana State Museum, by Pierre Joseph Landry. One (Fig. 24), carved of elm and stained dark, combines two heads joined and turned, Janus-like in opposite directions, with figured low reliefs on the sides. A plausible interpretation of the symbolism involved still awaits more detailed information as to the artist's beliefs and experience. It is possible that he is telling us something of the relation of master and servant, involving perhaps personal experience. Landry came from an aristocratic family that left France in 1785 shortly before the revolution; we do not know for what reasons. His family owned slaves in Louisiana. Two other wood carvings of elm wood combine figures in the round with reliefs on the base. These carvings are also symbolic in meaning and primitive in style. This is clearly a case where a self-trained amateur artist uses wood carving for purposes of self expression, by selecting themes that suggest a social consciousness, all truly ambitious ventures.

A bust said to be of Henry Clay,[9] carved in mahogany, stained dark, by an unknown carver, suggests a real person. With little or no training, the carver lacked the skill to realize what he had in mind to accomplish. McIntire, by comparison,

FIG. 24. *Symbolic group by Pierre Joseph Landry, from Iberville Parish, Louisiana.*

could cope with difficulties by falling back on a decorative manner with which he was familiar.

A Franklin bust, by Alexander Swasey (1784–1864) now in the United States Post Office at Newport, Rhode Island, suggests the competent professional carver.[10] The restraining influence of the wood made him deal with drapery in a simplified manner. The long curled hair and the scarf contrast effectively with forehead and cheeks. The bust with its pedestal is influenced by marble busts and is painted white.

There are innumerable paintings of George Washington and numerous marble and bronze statues and busts, but wood carvings of Washington are rare. One bust,[11] about three feet high, carved in pine and painted white (as of December, 1938) shows him in a simplified toga on a square base. The head is somewhat idealized, the hair is in long waves and the expression is one of power and aloofness. This is a dignified and handsome interpretation, close to a marble bust which is attributed to Joseph Nollekens[12] (1737–1823).

A figure of George Washington (Fig. 25) in uniform, blue coat and yellow breeches, is by another unknown carver. It uses a posture also used by John Quincy Adams Ward in his statue on the steps of the New York Subtreasury. The carver, like the folk artist that he is, makes the most of details, as in the epaulets, the sword and the curiously grooved pedestal. The wrinkles in Washington's vest fascinate him, and he is exact about the buttons. Details appeal to the folk artist, who is at heart a decorator. To be able to feel the human figure and, in addition, to incorporate an heroic element that belongs to Washington, is outside his province. Folk art understands what is concrete and deals admirably with the inanimate, but lacks the capacity to suggest life. Something of a doll-like character clings to its representation of the figure, which follows types and does not get beyond the surface. The study of anatomy requires a rigorous discipline; the folk carver wastes no time on it. He desires results; a reasonable likeness and a properly rendered uniform.

Another larger painted wooden statue of George Washington in uniform, by William Sullivan (1776), now at the Delaware Historical Society, stood in Bowling Green, New York City from

FIG. 25. *Figure of George Washington.*

1792 to 1843. At that time it disappeared from public view till 1889 when it reappeared temporarily. Before it was finally acquired by the Historical Society, it had served as a shop figure in New York City at three different addresses.

George Washington attracted folk artists as late as 1907, when A. L. Peterson, in Scandia, Minnesota, carved Washington[13] on horseback out of a mahogany board, stained dark, sixteen inches high and one inch thick, thinned down in places to one-half inch. With drawn sword, Washington is shown in front view, the horse in side view, placed on a leafy base. The composition is effective as a silhouette.

David G. Blythe[14] (1815–1865) of East Liverpool, Ohio, carved a figure of General Lafayette in walnut, eight feet high, which in 1945 still stood before the Fayette County Courthouse in Uniontown, Pennsylvania. Blythe was apprenticed to Joseph Woodwell, a wood carver in Pittsburgh. A figure of Civil War Union General John A. Dix[15] in blue uniform, about four feet high, was carved by Herman D. A. Henning of Baltimore, Maryland, about 1875. A small mahogany figure of William Penn,[16] about twenty inches high, is in the Philadelphia Museum.

A wooden Indian[17] who is not a sidewalk figure but a portrait, represents a well-known Osage chief, known as *Le Soldat du Chêne*, Soldier of the Oak, because of an encounter in which an oak tree furnished him a vantage point from which to resist his enemies. The statue was carved about 1805–1806, in Washington, D. C., on the occasion of the chief's visit to the capital, when, accompanied by Colonel Choteau of St. Louis, he visited President Thomas Jefferson. The statue of white cedar is life sized; including the base it is over six and one-half feet tall. It appears to be the work of an experienced sculptor.

An inn sign (Fig. 7) from New Hampshire,[18] carved in relief with a head, around 1800, may have been intended to represent the innkeeper. The artist may have been an architectural carver, judging from the skill he shows in the scroll border. He tried to adapt his linear techniques to the relief bust, so that this relief also takes on the character of ornament.

No systematic research seems to have been made on carved busts and reliefs. Talented youngsters who were interested in portraiture might have started with whittling and wood carving but eventually took up stone and marble. Even of those known to have started with wood carving, few early works have been identified.

Fig. 26. *Sternpiece from the* John Penrose, *nineteenth century.*

Ornamental figures were designed for places on buildings, or in connection with gardens and fountains. The courthouse was surmounted by a figure of Justice,[19] as in Worcester, Massachusetts; the post office at times had a flying Mercury, like one[20] over the door of the Boston Post Office in State Street, attributed to Simeon Skillin. In other instances, figures were designed for niches either for exterior decoration or for some special place within the building. A pediment of a public building might have in the center a shield or a gilt eagle. Today this type of monumental wood carving is mostly in private collections and in local historical societies.

The Skillin brothers,[21] Simeon (1757–1806) and John (1746–1800), were well-known wood carvers who worked on figureheads and ship carvings for the wealthy merchants of Boston. A garden figure, called Pomona, has something of the fashion of the eighteenth century, and was carved in 1793 by Simeon Skillin. The pose is pictorial, as if the carver had seen a picture that gave him this suggestion, and the skirt is arranged in almost symmetrical folds, which do not conform to the figure underneath the cloth. Mannerisms like stylized drapery, sloping shoulders, a heavy neck and fully rounded head are Skillin characteristics.

Though the Skillins carved many figures, few have been identified. On the basis of their style, a well-known but heretofore unidentified figure of Justice (see endpaper front), privately owned in Boston, is here attributed to the Skillins.[22] This figure is more attractive than either Pomona or the gilt Justice of the Worcester Historical Society,[23] also by the Skillins.

Of wood-carved figures of this type and period that have become known, this Boston-owned Justice is the best. The slender figure against the massive sword, lightly supported by the palm of her hand, is very effective. The heavy neck and sturdy arms add to a contrast of lightness against weight. The drapery is shaped into long folds that spread and separate as they descend, and is laid in parallel coils around the arms. It almost looks like rope; you feel the ship carver, heavy-handed but determined to be elegant. The figure is stilted, a support for drapery, with little organic feeling. She could be a little Bo-Peep, from Mother Goose; the hand that held the scales might also be about to wipe off a tear. Academic tradition and a folk expression combine to produce charm and individuality.

This figure must be by the Skillins, because it is the same in style, type of figure, motifs and carving, as three small figures on top of a chest of the Garvan Collection at Yale University.[24] The figures on the Garvan chest are like the Garden Figures now proved to be Skillins', hence the chest figures and also the Justice must be theirs too.

Justice dates from before July, 1806, when Isaac Fowle and Edmund Raymond took over the Skillin shop. With a companion figure of Hope, Justice occupied a niche on the façade of a Boston Custom House, the exact location of which is not known. Drake in his *Old Landmarks and Historic Personages of Boston* mentions these two figures. Both are fine examples of American wood carving of the period around 1800.

Hope[25] (see endpaper front), standing close to a large anchor, seems solid and compact compared to the open and loosely composed Justice, which is more readily recognizable as being by the Skillins. Presumably both statues are from the same shop, and it can hardly be said that one is artistically superior to the other.

A figure of Justice by John Fisher is believed to have been used indoors in a courtroom in York, Pennsylvania, about the time of the Revolution. It is about twenty-one inches high, and is privately owned.

There are other remains of early wood carvings in this category, though some examples are fragments only. A head wearing a helmet[26] is believed to be from a statue of Minerva, carved in 1822 by a wood carver by the name of Schafer, later anglicized to Shepherd, of Cincinnati, Ohio. The features are classic; the head is painted over a coating of gesso; the style is in the traditional manner of eighteenth-century craftsmanship. As interest turns in this direction, it may be expected that other as yet not generally known examples may come to light, as one that Powers is said to have carved for Cincinnati.

Two female reliefs,[27] near life size, privately owned, in a reclining posture as if intended as flanking figures on either side of a central feature, may be by Joseph Wilson, around 1810, a carver of Newburyport, Massachusetts. One holds a horn of plenty, the other a laurel branch. Academic and folk-art manners again combine effectively in these unusual reliefs. They are believed to have been owned by Timothy Dexter, the well-known eccentric eighteenth-century merchant of Newburyport.

A fragment of a Flying Mercury,[28] once part of a weathervane, is an eighteenth-century piece from the Royall House garden in Medford, Massachusetts. The tall, slender figure, nine feet high, uses a static pose, as the carver was constrained by the shape of the tree trunk. The missing leg, once attached separately, suggested action. Little drapery is left, and you wonder how this fragment might have been completed. Perhaps a figurehead carver derived the motif from historic art, for the maker was a trained craftsman, familiar with the art of the past. The Mercury now has a weathered surface which is pleasing in itself, in addition to the sensitive modeling of the torso, in the manner of classic sculpture. The head is tilted back; the cheeks are heavy and the hair is in broad masses. What is left of the figure shows a fine quality.

In another standing figure,[29] in the Rhode Island School of Design, one feels the heavy hand of the figurehead carver. The figure holds a bouquet in her bent right hand. Feet and pedestal are missing, but though mutilated, the figure has considerable charm.

A nineteenth-century garden figure (see endpaper back),[30] a half-nude figure of a girl caressing a bird, is a Victorian descendant of an eighteenth-century motif. The bird is perhaps a turtle dove, alluding to Venus, goddess of love, whose chariot was drawn by doves. The parted hair with a knot in the back, the drapery and the ivory color (July, 1937) to suggest marble, are in the classicizing taste of the period. From whatever source the carver may have obtained assistance, the bunched-up folds of cloth may indicate that he had largely drawn on his own resources. Though technically ill-equipped for the purposes of academic art, the carver had an abundance of determination and faith in himself to carry through a figure about five feet high. More recently, in 1939, this figure was repainted in "Pompeian red"; in December, 1940, the figure showed up in flesh color, blue drapery and dark blue base.[31]

The life cycle of a larger wood carving begins when it is created out of a log in the carver's shop. It spends its youth in honorable service, fulfilling the purpose for which it was created; admired, or at least accepted. If it survives the destruction of its habitat through shipwreck, fire or building demolition, the carving may be thrown aside in the lumber-yard of some wrecking concern. From here it may be rescued to find a temporary lodging in the shop of an antique dealer. At this stage the carving may receive repairs or alterations, but it may still be stored in a backyard. When at last discovered by a collector, the carving may continue an outdoor existence; sometimes in a garden, where it may feel at home, because some figures were originally designed for gardens, as Simeon Skillin's Pomona.[30] Most of the larger figures were made for the out-of-doors. Figureheads seem to be drawn to shady garden nooks, projecting out from a tree and held in place by a length of strap iron. All too often, however, such carvings are found in inappropriate environments; stuck against the clapboard or stucco walls of modern houses. Eventually the fortunate ones reach a haven of safety in a museum.

This is particularly true of large statues that require space, but almost invariably a dealer or collector takes over before such pieces come into public ownership. This happened recently when a lover of Americana[31] acquired a more-than-life-sized wooden figure of a coal miner just as it was being covered over permanently in connection with some filling-in operation on an industrial site in Louisville, Kentucky. This miner with a pick over his shoulder, from around 1890 or earlier, stood out of doors in the midst of a flower garden. Such a figure is truly wood sculpture in the sense that it served as a public monument and as a memorial as well.

Not all wooden figures look like shop figures; sometimes they look like sculpture. The New York State Historical Association at Cooperstown has an outstanding wood-carved figure of a Negro preacher, known as Reverend Campbell. He wears a vermilion coat and holds a satchel in one hand, an umbrella in the other. Simplicity of form with spectacular color make this figure noteworthy. The same museum has another impressive figure, unique among all others. In her left hand she holds cigars, which makes her a shop figure. More significant is the fact that we have here power and refinement rarely equaled elsewhere. The fact that she holds cigars seems incidental to her larger purpose of having been created as a distinguished monument. It is believed to have been carved by a Negro slave in the early nineteenth century.

A small seated Liberty (Plate XII), only three feet high, is also a true memorial, for it enthrones Liberty the way a religious image would be seated to confront a worshipper. With a slight change in the posture of the arms, the Liberty would become a Madonna. It reflects the artist's familiarity with the religious art of Italy. Perhaps the artist aspired to the academic art of his native land and fused this with a striving for a free American expression. The two books must symbolize learning and presumably refer to the freedom of education in the artist's adopted country. The dog may be a pet animal. The inscriptions, "Liberty" and the "United States of America," the star on the belt of the figure, together with the artist's own signature at the base suggest that the artist identified himself with the liberty of his new country, symbolized by the whole figure. Here, as in the case of the Landry carving, a newcomer to this country becomes a folk artist and uses wood carving symbolically; a work of art becomes a confession of faith.

# CHAPTER IV

# DECORATION

Architectural carving between early Colonial times and the late nineteenth century may be broadly differentiated by centuries. During the seventeenth century, carving elaborated structural members, but hardly existed in its own right. The eighteenth century through the early Federal period brought architectural wood carving to its finest flowering. Throughout the nineteenth century, architecture outgrew the era of handicrafts without integrating harmoniously into the machine age, and the significance of wood carving was reduced.

In the seventeenth-century Colonial house, the heavy wooden frames were given a modest decorative treatment. Chamfered and molded posts and beams, carved drop ornaments at the second-story level, as well as occasional carved verge boards (the exterior rafters finishing off the gables) constituted about the only carved parts of the house. As the medieval character of the frame house gave way to eighteenth-century classic design, wood carving found new opportunities in carved moldings, friezes, panels, brackets and capitals. On the exterior, the portal might be elaborated with carved brackets over carved pilasters as in the case of Dummer Academy of Byfield, Massachusetts (1715).[1] The panel over the door of the Lady Pepperell House (c. 1760) of Kittery Point, Maine, has two symmetrically arranged dolphins ending in leafy tails in the robust manner of the ship carver.[2] The same motif reappears on a South Parlor mantel of the Governor John Wentworth House (c. 1769) at Portsmouth, New Hampshire.[3]

Designs for chimneypieces and doorways were derived from

various handbooks printed in England and in this country for the use of architect-builders. Abraham Swan's *British Architect or Builders' Treasury etc.* (after 1745) and *The Country Builder's Assistant* by Asher Benjamin (1798 and earlier) are examples. Individual master carpenters followed the design so closely that it has been possible to point to the exact pages in one of these engraved books from which well-known designs have been copied. The chimneypiece in the Council Chamber of the Governor Wentworth House at Little Harbor, New Hampshire, near Portsmouth, is derived from plate 64 in William Kent's *Designs of Inigo Jones.*[4]

But there are also local variations in the way moldings were cut, and reeding, fluting and gouge work were interpreted. Sometimes the carver may have misunderstood the line drawings of his guide book and inadvertently made a change where he thought he was following the book.

Motifs reproduced in the builders' books, intended for stone, plaster or composition, were carved in wood.[5]

This carving is in connection with mantels, keystones, door trims, window casings, stairways and wainscots. Fine examples are found from Maine to South Carolina.[6] A carved walnut frieze (c. 1730) around a stairwell at Tuckahoe, Virginia, is of superior craftsmanship, showing, in the breadth of the scrolled leaves and flowers[7] a resemblance to seventeenth-century Dutch furniture carving. Balusters and newel posts of the staircases were elaborately turned and the ends of the treads carved with console-like scrolls. In one example the main newel post contains a carved double spiral, the inner one turning in an opposite direction from the outer one.[8]

Samuel McIntire[9] of Salem, Massachusetts, of the early Federal period, is known particularly for his carved mantels. His carved moldings and his ornamental panels, with carved baskets of fruits, garlands and sheaves of wheat have been justly admired and praised for their delicacy. Stimulated by the Adam style in England, as it came to his attention through engraved book illustrations, McIntire developed a carving style of his own. He also used cast composition ornaments after the English manner; which were usually imported, but on occasion cast from his own carvings.[10]

The basket with fruit is one of his most individual carvings. Even though the general idea of basket or dish of fruit may have come to McIntire from the illustrated handbooks, his varied designs, exquisitely carved, are his own contribution. He also used musical instruments, festoons of drapery, sprays of grape, laurel, horns of plenty and eagles.[11] Wood carving as a part of the interior decoration of the home never achieved the same significance elsewhere as in these McIntire houses in Salem.

The eighteenth century produced some carving for fence- and gateposts. A gatepost decoration (Fig. 27) may bear some relation to the type of phoenix ornament on top of Chippendale gilt mirror frames. Ornithologically speaking, judging from head, beak and toes, this bird suggests a chicken. As such, the anatomy is reasonably correct, except for the feathers. They are made into a pattern, with each feather enlarged. The craftsman in wood exaggerates the thickness of details that can be seen in nature but not felt. He appeals to our tactile sense and less to vision. This carving is by an experienced artisan who knew the traditions of his craft and may have worked for cabinetmakers. It is now in the Newport Rhode Island Historical Society. It is dated 1750, and thus antedates the American eagle.

Examples of eagles are found along the Atlantic seaboard from north to south, as in an eagle over the doorway of the Goshen, Connecticut, Library[12] of 1824. A gilded eagle[13] carved in oak within the pediment of the South Carolina National Bank (1816–1817) in Charleston, South Carolina, is effective in silhouette and vigorous in detail.

A carved overdoor decoration, eagle and crossed flags (Fig. 28) from the Old Custom House in Rockland, Maine, was carved (1865) by Joseph Verrill[14] in the ship carvers' tradition. Dissimilar elements—eagle, flags and scrolls—are unified. In the center all shapes come together in a lively, well-ordered manner. The small texture of the wings and the grooved texture of the flags contrast pleasantly. Note the spiky leaves, the vigorous turns, the sharp edges, so characteristic of the acanthus foliage and so much a part of the European tradition.

Carved cats' heads (c. 1800) once forming the end of the

PLATE VII. *"Colonel Sellers," Apothecary Figure, 1875.*

PLATE VIII. *Cigar-store Indian, nineteenth century.*

FIG. 27. *Fence post ornament,*
*gilt eagle, c. 1750.*

booms which were used on the bows of sailing vessels as derricks
on which to raise the anchor, were temporarily used on houses
and barns before they were turned over to the Historical Society.[15] A boar's head[16] found attached to the end of a hay-joist
belongs to this group of incidental architectural wood carving.

Edbury Hatch[17] (1849–1935) of Newcastle, Maine, had been
a ship carver, working for William Southworth of Newcastle,
and for Colonel Charles A. L. Sampson of Bath, Maine, who, as
we recall, carved the figureheads for the *Belle of Bath* and per-

FIG. 28. *Eagle with Crossed Flags and* E Pluribus Unum *Banderole, c. 1865, from Old Customs House, Portland, Maine. By Joseph Verrill.*

haps the *White Lady*. When ship carving as an occupation became a thing of the past, Hatch kept on working for his pleasure, carving decorations for his own house. One of them (Fig. 29), a gutter spout, made to shed the rain water away from the house, represents the head of a fabulous monster. Four influences fuse in this carving: a horse's mouth, shark's teeth, a recollection of a gargoyle from a French cathedral, and ornamental leaf carving. These motifs mingle to produce a design that is original and based as much on invention as on archeology. These carvings grew out of native Maine figurehead carving. They are now privately owned in Newcastle, Damariscotta and Wiscasset.

Even during the eighteenth century carvings on the outside of the house were never profuse. As the Classic revival of the early nineteenth century was replaced by the Gothic revival, the jigsaw replaced chisel and gouge. Few houses escaped entirely; at least the porch was embellished with some scroll work. Among the spectacular examples are the *Wedding Cake House* at Kennebunkport, Maine,[18] and the *Lace House* at Blackhawk, Colorado.[19] Typically American was the application of this style to the interiors of river steamboats in the so-

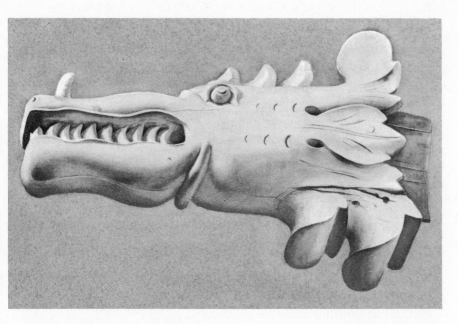

Fig. 29. *Ornament, Gargoyle, carved by Edbury Hatch at Newcastle, Maine.*

called "Steamboat Gothic."[20] The salon of the *Great Republic* was fantastic in its splendor of carved wood brackets on either side of a row of chandeliers, recalling a cathedral nave, in which length rather than height assured effect.

During the period of transition from craft to industry, design often deteriorated. As power replaced handwork, some crafts declined and the continuity of a single tradition was interrupted. A change in taste was responsible for an insistence on realism and a display of skill with a corresponding loss of vigor. This is illustrated in ornate mantelpieces in the late Victorian period. A dog's head carved in high relief and crowded into the spandrel of an arch shows details to excess, down to a deceptively real collar complete with buckle.[21]

Carving, like much of nineteenth-century design, was retrospective. An over-mantel mirror frame might be carved in Circassian walnut in an adaptation of the Rococo manner and made complete with the Medici arms of Florence.[22] How the mantel of the city mansion of 1890 was carved depended on the land of origin of the carver, and on the particular historical style the architect was adapting. It might be in the style of the French Louis Quinze or Louis Seize, Northern Renaissance or Modern English.[23]

One aspect of this period is the separation between the designer who copied something on the drafting board and an artisan who followed a blueprint. When carving was no longer the work of one mind, but divided among the original European style, the draftsman-designer-copyist and a carver, it lost its meaning and became at best an ornamental extravagance.

Among the earliest wood carvings on furniture are the carved desk-boxes and chests from New England, a few dated in the last quarter of the seventeenth century. As outposts of European culture, these household luxuries may reflect in design a particular locality of England or Holland. The motifs used were limited in number and were restricted geographically, as in the cases of Hadley and Hartford chests.

Fine examples of carved boxes are in the Metropolitan, Brooklyn and Boston museums of art.[24] Small rectangular boxes from Connecticut have fronts and sometimes the sides carved. The designs on the front show two or three lunettes, semicircles, with gouged-out borders repeating the semicircles and incised pine cones and tulips filling in the spaces. It is an economical type of decoration in which a good deal of the original surface of the board remains untouched. In others, the background is carved out, allowing the design to stand out in the original surface of the wood. The wood surface receives an additional enrichment from the tiger-like markings of the quarter-sawed oak, that shows up light against a background dotted with tool marks. In this technique all-over patterns of symmetrically disposed tulips are used. A solid border is left standing in the original surface so that the decoration forms a panel, which adds to sturdiness and protects the carving. An elaborately carved desk-box is in the Brooklyn Museum.[25] It shows chip-carved designs of wheels, rosettes and hearts, and is perhaps of Dutch (Friesland) inspiration.

Related to the boxes of this period are the larger chests in which the earliest designs are of English derivation, as they occur on Elizabethan and Jacobean mantelpieces and wall panelings.[26] An oak chest[27] of the third quarter of the seventeenth century shows an extraordinary richness. Stiles, rails and three panels are covered with a guilloche, laurel, rectangle, circle, rosette and palm leaf design. The panels are carved with leaf and tulip motifs that, tree-like, fill in each panel to produce magnificent patterns, of English inspiration; later ones belong more definitely to New England. One from Ipswich, Massachusetts, has been attributed to Thomas Dennis (d. 1706).

A few designs in combinations are used repeatedly on chests, cupboards and wainscot chairs during the seventeenth century;[28] an examination of the wood, if nothing else, may determine whether a carved chest is of American or English make.

A well-known carved oak chest[29] with a signature of the maker, Nicholas Disbrowe, shows conventionalized tulips and leaves on rails, stiles and panels, adaptations of English designs. As Disbrowe is also a Dutch name, the designs may be Dutch importations into England. On a variation of the Disbrowe type of panel design appear large rosettes, also called asters or sunflowers. This type occurs frequently; it was made at Hartford or vicinity[30] (Fig. 30).

FIG. 30. *Chest from Hartford, c. 1700.*

Carved chests from Hadley, Massachusetts,[31] have a character of their own. A leaf, flower and scroll pattern repeats over the entire surface. Three panels recessed between stiles contain each a symmetrical motif of sprays of the same design or two palm leaves. The initials of the owner may be carved into the central panel.

John Allis, a carpenter of Hatfield, Massachusetts, made a chest[32] for his daughter Elizabeth, which carries her initial, E.A., in the outer oak panels. This chest[33] is believed to have formed the model for subsequent Hadley chests, made and carved by the firm of Belden and Allis. The tulip border of the top rail of the Disbrowe chest may have influenced the Hadley chests. The prevalence of carved chests attests to a will for artistic expression. Linked to customs and family traditions, this desire to transcend a purely utilitarian level of living must have been strong to persist in a frontier country filled with hardships and insecurity.

Hanging spoon racks[34] with attached knife boxes are almost the only carved utensils. They are notched to hold a dozen pewter spoons. The chip-carved decoration is of the Frisian type and includes spiral wheels, stars, sunbursts and rising suns, as well as tulip motifs. The spoon racks have been traced to the Hudson and Delaware river valleys, northern Jersey and Pennsylvania, the regions of Dutch, Swedish and German settlers. We may assume that they are native American eighteenth-century survivals of North European ancestry; as in Europe these racks were made by the groom for the bride, as love tokens.

For the better part of the seventeenth century, furniture was scarce and was mostly utilitarian; chest, box and wainscot chair were the only pieces of carved furniture, if we overlook the turned legs of chairs and tables. Panel and stile construction encouraged flat surface decoration. Carved wainscot chairs that formerly were believed to be English have more recently been claimed for Thomas Dennis of Ipswich, Massachusetts. A fine example of his is the Pilgrim Chair[35] of the Essex Institute at Salem.

With the appearance of the bannister-back chair in the last quarter of the seventeenth century, the backs were scroll-carved to form a crest.[36] There was some carving in Queen Anne furniture, in the early eighteenth century, and carving became conspicuous during the following Chippendale period. The crest rail of the back with its boldly scrolled ears, the carved knees of the legs and carved shells of the centers of back and seat frame, and the carved claw-and-ball feet reach a high degree of elegance, in the Philadelphia Chippendale chair of the third quarter of the eighteenth century.[37] Though various craftsmen contributed to their excellence, few names have been related to specific chairs. Benjamin Randolph and James Gillingham have been identified because chairs with their labels have been found. One of the finest of side chairs in the M. and M. Karolik Collection of the Boston Museum of Fine Arts[38] bears no label. In the design of the chair, carving and proportion are of equal importance and combine to achieve distinction.

To appreciate this eighteenth-century restraint in a carved chair, it should be compared with a carved rosewood armchair of the mid-nineteenth century by John Henry Belter.[39] In this very pretentious chair, every portion of the wooden frame is elaborated with curves, scrolls, leaves, flowers and grapes. And yet this piece of decoration for the sake of elaboration is consistent and well designed. The Post-Civil War period produced such an abundance of bad taste that the style as a whole is more blamed than praised.

Returning to the eighteenth century of the period immediately preceding the Revolution, we find the most florid carving on top of Philadelphia highboys in the central cartouche placed between the carved rosette ends of the pediment.[40] Fine examples[41] are in the American Wing of the Metropolitan Museum, like one with a pierced top beneath the scrolls, a central carved bust and carved corner urns. This piece and a lowboy, a companion piece, are believed to be by Benjamin Randolph. Another dressing table or lowboy,[42] differing in the details of the carving, which is more closely packed with scrollwork, has been attributed to another Philadelphia craftsman, William Savery.

Of equal excellence is the carving in two Philadelphia dressing tables[43] owned by the Boston Museum of Fine Arts; the wood being San Domingo mahogany richly grained.

These craftsmen worked with a limited number of conventional motifs that had long been a part of an established tradition. Variations were along the line of perfecting and refining familiar forms. Exquisite taste combined with excellent craftsmanship produced superior results. On occasion the versatility of an individual carver brought forth startling results, admirable at least for the boldness of the attempt. An example is a carved portrait head in place of the finial on top of a walnut secretary from Pennsylvania (c. 1760), between the pediment scrolls. The carving of the head in simple folk-art manner is still out of keeping in this place.[44]

For the period after the Revolution, Samuel McIntire of Salem is known to us from his carved portraits and mantelpieces, but he was also a furniture carver.[45] He used rosettes, crossed horns of plenty, dishes of fruit and edges of reeding similar to those found on his mantels in his Salem houses. A signed sketch in the Essex Institute of Salem makes it plausible that he carved a handsome back of a chair[46] made by Benjamin Frothingham of Charlestown, Massachusetts.

The Chippendale style produced finely carved shells of blockfront kneehole desks and chests, as in one by Edmund Townsend of Newport, Rhode Island.[47] Blocks of mahogany are here embellished with carved semicircular shells which are extraordinary in their precision, sweep and elegance. In the furniture of Duncan Phyfe[48] (1757–1854?) the carving of table legs, chair and bedposts and pedestals becomes flat and delicate. The perfectly executed acanthus leaf often used is reduced to alternate grooves and ridges. One of his chairs in the Metropolitan Museum, made for DeWitt Clinton, has a carved spread eagle as a back.

The mahogany carved and gilt New England mirrors[49] of the Chippendale style in the third quarter of the eighteenth century produced an exuberant variety of designs, in which carving (Fig. 31) has much to contribute.[50] One of many fine examples is a carved oval mirror surmounted by a phoenix or pheasant and enclosed on the outer oval by a series of delicate acanthus leaves. It was carved by John Welch (d. 1789), the carver of the famed sacred codfish in the Boston State House.[51]

FIG. 31. *Mirror from Philadelphia. Mahogany veneer, c. 1775.*

American furniture carving[52] at its finest and in its greatest variety can be studied and appreciated in the comprehensive collection of the Henry Francis DuPont Winterthur Museum. Every kind is represented, including various superb examples in the Chippendale manner. There are choice pieces, each type culminating in examples that represent carving at its best. A mahogany Philadelphia sidechair shows with what freedom and good taste the American craftsman translated a Chippendale engraving into a chair of wood. The Connecticut block-front style is well represented in a cherry chest-of-drawers.[53] Perhaps the ultimate is achieved in the richly carved high chests-of-drawers of the Philadelphia school of the period immediately preceding and coinciding with the Revolution. Here the carving is exuberant and yet restrained, so that every detail is beautiful in itself, and merges with the whole design.[54]

American eighteenth-century furniture carving competed for the patronage of a small group of merchants and planters who were familiar with European standards. That competition produced high level achievements along established lines.

Carving is a handcraft and does not lend itself to mass production by machines. The spirit of the nineteenth century as it progressed was therefore not congenial to its growth. Where furniture was carved, it was at times the incidental work of a craftsman who spent his leisure hours to carve pieces for his own use. Such carvers often excel in skill but are deficient in taste. Without the discipline of competition, such carvings may reflect the less attractive side of the Victorian manner. Newspaper racks to hang on the wall, towel racks, comb and brush racks, clock shelves, corner brackets, gun racks and hall racks belong to this group.[55] Nevertheless, not all carved walnut is in poor taste. Proof of this is a well-designed oval dressing table mirror frame (Fig. 32) made in Cincinnati about 1850.[56]

Occasionally, pieces of furniture, like chairs, come to light where a craftsman has added carving of his own to a traditional type of chair. The combination results in unorthodox designs, that nevertheless have merit. A convict in a Kentucky penitentiary around 1870 produced an armchair in oak with turned front legs and turned spindles to which he added a richly carved back splat.[57] In another case, the carver placed a pierced back between turned uprights.[58]

During the second half of the nineteenth century, a school of wood carving flourished in Cincinnati, Ohio, due in large measure to the fact that two English wood carvers settled there.

FIG. 32. *Dressing table mirror, walnut, by M. L. Duncan and Brother, Cincinnati, Ohio, c. 1850.*

William H. Fry (1830–1929) was the English-born son of a noted wood carver of Bath, England, Henry L. Fry. The father, Henry, who trained under Pugin, Barry and Scott, had carved the throne chair of Queen Victoria, and later chairs for Jenny Lind's first appearance in Cincinnati. Working in a modern

continuation of Ghiberti's naturalism of the Italian early Renaissance, the Frys raised wood carving to a high artistry through
professional work and teaching at the Cincinnati Art School. At
the time of the Civil War, William assisted his father Henry,
who had come to Cincinnati in 1851, with the carving on the
grand staircase of the old Henry Probasco home in Cincinnati.
Residences, churches, stores, public buildings were carved by
William Fry, as well as Baldwin pianos, church candlesticks,
and many smaller objects. He took his motifs from flowers and
birds and gave to historic forms, particularly the acanthus
motifs, a delicate sensitive beauty. When the qualities of the
nineteenth-century style come into their own, the charm and
grace of the Fry school of wood carving should take high rank.

In 1873 Benn Pitman (d. 1910), the brother of Sir Isaac Pitman of stenographic fame, started out at the Cincinnati Art
Academy to teach a class of sixty women practical designing
and wood carving. Benn Pitman took up wood carving, which
was fashionable in the early eighties, in Cincinnati. For two
decades, from 1885 to 1905, he carved the interior of a house
built for his son, its fireplaces, organ loft, stairway, doors, using
motifs of grapes and leaves of oak, leaving no surface untouched.
The carving is in low relief on the baseboards, for sake of pro-
tection. On the doorstile carving is sunk, but at higher levels
high relief is used. The motifs are floral, gained from the local
Ohio flora.

The Frys and Pitman carried on the craftsman's tradition of
wood carving in a cultured art school environment. The wood
is black walnut, which has turned dark through the application
of crude oil and turpentine.

In the Spanish Southwest, particularly in Southern California, we find carved furniture. In the late eighteenth and early
nineteenth centuries wood carving served the practical needs of
furnishing the mission church. This exists in two versions,
which might be called native and Spanish.

The native furniture[59] also shows the Spanish influence,
though carved by Mission Indians under the direction of the
padres. It consists of wall-stands, baptismal fonts, candelabra,
confessionals, crosses, lintels, missal stands, niches, pedestals,

tabernacles and related objects. Properly speaking these pieces
owe more to the saw than the chisel. Carving in the sense of
carving in relief or in the round hardly exists; carving is
scratched or incised; the scale is large; forms are heavy and surfaces broad. A European origin is recognizable, but the style
has been flattened and simplified. A carved missal stand or an
ecclesiastic candlestick[60] or an ornamental gate[61] show how carving has changed, at the hands of the natives to whom the European designs were unfamiliar.

Pulpits[62] and confessionals[63] have paneled sides, each panel
(Fig. 33) ornamented with carved rosettes or shaped or rectangular plaques. Crescents, circles and straight line borders are
gouged out of flat boards. Later missions like Santa Ines (1814)
and Santa Barbara (1820) may have profited from the experi-
ences of earlier missions of the same region in matters of decoration. The padres and their Indian assistants presumably combined forces. The California Indians were excellent basket
makers, but they are not known to have had any native wood
carving of their own. The wood-carved decorations that are

FIG. 33. *Confessional, detail, c. 1809. Carved by Indian Neophyte.*

ascribed to them were conceived in the minds of their mission teachers. It is said that the carving was left to Indian neophytes. But this was not always the case; carvers of European origin, perhaps from Mexico, Spain or New England may also have participated. Such a person may have carved the panel showing a spray of wild roses, in which conventionalized roses combine well with less conventionalized leaves, buds and stems. This panel, measuring two feet eight inches, was rescued from a rubbish heap at Santa Barbara Mission[64] after the earthquake of 1925.

Incised carving using spiral, crescents and thumbnail motifs were used on the horizontal back splats and aprons of armchairs.[65] The rectangular, Spanish Renaissance type of armchair made entirely of posts and rails was still used in California missions in the early nineteenth century. In the simplest carved version of this type only rows of thumbnail motifs occur.[66] Those chairs with shaped and carved stretchers in front were imported,[67] and the plainer carved stretcher type may have been too.

Classical motifs (Fig. 34) reached Mexico through Spain, from where they traveled north and became a part of the Cali-

Fig. 34. *Lunette, leaves and scrolls, from Santa Ines Mission, c. 1804.*

fornia Mission vocabulary. In the hands of an Indian who worked on a lunette at Santa Ines Mission, classical leaves and scrolls took on a new flavor. All sharpness has been softened and made into more nearly abstract shapes.

If we remember that the native Indian of Southern California has been described as a leisurely person, bent mostly on eating and sleeping, we might conjecture that this type of carving is a reflection of the Indian's easy way of life.

European peasant influences have on occasion found expression in furniture. These were incidental and, short-lived contributions, with few remaining examples to illustrate. A Swedish "Kubbstob"[68] or block chair, an early primitive type (Fig. 35) was carved in 1840 in Racine, Wisconsin. It consists of a hollowed-out section of a tree trunk, with a flat seat and curved back left standing in the outer wood of the trunk. The chair is by no means as clumsy looking as might be surmised from the simplicity of the structure.[69]

Fig. 35. *Wooden log chair, c. 1840, by Hans Ellerdson in Norway (Racine), Wisconsin.*

# CHAPTER V

# HOUSEHOLD ARTICLES

For the few carvers who undertook life-sized statues there were many who were satisfied with smaller carvings.[1] Two types of small object carvers may be distinguished, those who were settled on the land, artisans and farmers, by far the larger group; and occasional migratory workers. The first group produced objects for which there was a demand, like butter molds, toys, small and large; decoys and weathervanes. It includes a professional carver and the folk artist. Together they have produced most of the carvings in this category.

The second group consisted of leisure-time, migratory workers, like sailors,[2] lumberjacks and "forty-niners," men whose strenuous activity was interrupted by periods of enforced idleness. Often isolated, they were thrown back upon their own resources for amusement. Occasionally a whittler would turn his talents to carving, and at least a few examples have been preserved. Every lumberjack carried a jackknife, but only the exceptional individual developed his whittling sufficiently to become a folk artist.

A design transferred to wood and carved is often a motif that the carver has seen and remembered. It may be carved out of his head or it may be copied from a book. Wood carvers were probably unconscious of any desire to create something that posterity would herald as original. We must be prepared to find European motifs continued in American woods, applied to the kind of objects the carver was accustomed to, from his European background. It takes time before old habits are modified to create a new style. As the mode of living changed, some objects

PLATE IX. *Whirligig, "Sailor Jack," eighteenth century.*

went out of fashion before any appreciable stylistic change had time to manifest itself. Sometimes one can tell from the kind of object that it is European. This is true of elaborate treenware, and of small luxury articles, like ornately carved spoons, pie-crust wheels, stay-busks for corset bodices, lace bobbins, knitting sheaths, all products of leisure, intended as love gifts of the groom to his bride. American wood carving is apt to be utilitarian, and it is largely without the time-consuming elaboration which ill-fitted the strenuous life of the pioneer. Even the weathervane fulfilled a purpose, and whatever was carved was done for more than a show of skill.

An important group of small wood carvings consists of intaglio-carved butter molds,[3] well known in England and continental Europe, particularly in Switzerland. The simplest type of butter mold is the handstamp, round or segmental in shape, with or without a knob. They were turned out on a lathe, mold and knob being in one piece. The flat or slightly concave disk bottom was then carved with an incised design, so that when it was pressed into the butter it left a decoration in relief. The design also served to identify, in the market, the butter of a particular farmer or dairy.

It is believed that some early butter molds were home-made, whittled with a jackknife by the more handy farmers during long winter evenings, and that only later were they turned out by professionals using carving tools. By 1870 the use of various kinds of butter molds as trademarks was common.[4] Farmers purchased molds and "outfits" for printing butter from traveling salesmen[5] as late as 1880.

Many of the butter molds are remarkably good as designs. The one illustrated (Fig. 36) from Pennsylvania, shows a large heart with a circle filled with a fine net pattern and surrounded by notched borders. The formerly well-defined shapes, enhanced by clean cutting, are now worn down through use. Butter molds offered the artisan his opportunity. Chip carving, with a V-shaped cut, was used; the technique presented no great difficulties, and the design was necessarily simple.

The designs vary, but the types repeat; floral shapes, tulips, leaves, acorns, strawberries, pineapples, sheaves of wheat, roost-

FIG. 36. *Butter mold, Pennsylvania German.*

ers, cows, eagles, stars and hearts were popular. A variety of woods, soft and hard, were used, including poplar, pine, cherry, beech, maple and black walnut.

Two groups[6] stand out. One group shows symmetrical designs, vigorous, compact and with little background showing; the other, unsymmetrical designs, free and open in the spacing of details, with the background definitely in evidence. It has been suggested that the closed type is of a continental European derivation, and is found particularly in Pennsylvania. The open type seems to occur more often in New England, and may represent a New England interpretation of an English tradition.

Wood-carved blocks, somewhat resembling butter molds, were used by tailors in pressing and steaming. An example,[7] probably from Pennsylvania, is in the Chester County (Pennsylvania) Historical Society. It is about six inches long, of pine, and carved with a heart and floral design. The carving is vigorous; the surface is rough and shows awl holes for the escape of steam.

Wood blocks, cut in relief for the stamping of textile patterns, belong to this group of small wood carvings. Relief-carved blocks were also made for stamping grain sacks; one from Pennsylvania shows a design of heart and tulip with the initials B.E.[8]

Relief-carved maple sugar molds,[9] made of bass wood, are known in a long plank-like type. A specimen of about 1850, twenty-six inches by two and a half inches, was traced to the original owner. Originally it was longer and still shows nine different designs, leaf and heart shaped, carved with boldness and precision in a craftsmanlike manner.

Far more elaborate and on a truly monumental scale are a number of New York state marzipan or cake celebration molds of the first half of the nineteenth century. They are rectangular mahogany boards, intaglio-carved, from fourteen to thirty inches long, and of considerable artistic and historic interest. The area filled in with ornamental details is approximately oval-shaped, leaving the corners free. The designs show the skill of experienced carvers, professionally engaged in a craft. One,[10] created in memory of the defeat of Cornwallis, has the inscription "York Town 1781" and the name W. Farmer. W. Farmer, a New York City baker, was listed in the New York City directory repeatedly between 1815 and 1843. At the time of Lafayette's visit to this country, in 1824, ceremonial marzipan cakes were popular. One[11] shows Lafayette on horseback and the inscription, "General Lafayette the defender of French and American Liberty," surrounded by a wreath and two cornucopias filled with sprays of ivy and roses. It is distinguished in the richness of its pattern and the ease with which scroll and floral motifs are filled in around the central medallion. A spread eagle surmounts the rider. "Henry F. Cox, carver, 1824" is cut into the edge.

A fire engine is shown on a board[12] bearing the inscription "Manhattan"; on another[13] is a man in kilts between thistle and rose, flanked by bundles of wheat. For design and craftsmanship, these cake molds are superior.

Pennsylvania German intaglio-carved springerle boards are molds for the Christmas baking season, when small hard cookies, *springerle*, and soft honey cakes, *lebkuchen*, were produced in quantity. The dough was pressed into the mold and in that way given a decoration that came out as a relief. The smaller boards for one, two or even six cakes are from Lancaster County,

Pennsylvania, and Ashland County, Ohio;[14] they are of native workmanship. Even larger ones, containing as many as sixteen or twenty designs, that look as if they might be German importations, are known to have been carved in this country.[15] One of them was carved by Karl Linss in Missouri, around 1835. He was schoolteacher, farmer, bed and spinningwheel maker. The designs, representing figures, animal and vegetable motifs, expertly carved, clearly point to an established tradition.

Wooden toys[16] might be divided into dolls and all other forms of wooden toys, some of which were also carved. One doll,[17] a rare example, is in the Philadelphia Museum. It is about thirteen inches high and is carved out of a solid piece of wood, including the arms that are held out from the body but not carved separately. The little figure represents a lady in hoop skirt and tight bodice. According to a letter from the last owner, she was the property of Sarah Horn, aged seven in 1776, and was the work of a Philadelphia craftsman. She may be a miniature replica of Sarah herself, to be placed on the mantel, rather than a practical doll with which Sarah was allowed to play. The heavy-handed bulky manner points to a ship carver used to working in a large scale.

A more functional type of doll[18] (Fig. 37), about sixteen inches long, has a wooden head and shoulders and a rag body. The head shows only the bare contours and a slightly projecting nose. This homemade doll left a good deal to the imagination, but permitted the use of a real hand-sewn wardrobe. This type of doll, a primitive but native product, must have remained in use throughout the first half of the nineteenth century, even after more advanced types came in from abroad. An example[19] dated about 1845, twenty-two inches tall, has been preserved at the Confederate Museum in Richmond, Virginia. A mechanically superior type of jointed wooden doll came originally from Germany and Switzerland in the first half of the nineteenth century. This "Dutch doll," or "penny wooden," has been preserved in numerous examples.[20] Arms and legs were mere pegs, joined to a thicker plug that served as a body. These high-waisted mannikins were nevertheless elegant ladies; they served, rack-like, as a support for clothes. Such dolls were not only mobile in the joints, but could be set to hold any posture.

FIG. 37. *Doll with wooden head and shoulders.*

A further development of this jointed peg doll was a machine-carved realistic baby doll, with ball and socket joints, held together with steel shafts and springs.[21] Mechanically these dolls are more perfect, but artistically they lack the appeal of the long, graceful lines of the earlier dolls. A slightly more elegant version of the commercial doll is illustrated in an advertisement of the Jointed Doll Company of Springfield, Vermont, of about 1884.[22]

In 1859 James Rich of Redford, Ohio, carved two dolls[23] out of maple and polished the surface to an even smoothness that shows the clean whiteness of the wood. Here in "Emma" and "Jim," we have the true folk artist who works for an attainable goal and bestows upon it all the skill of which he is capable. Correct anatomy is not even attempted. Instead, simple shapes, cylindrical and oval, a fine surface and a respect for the beauty of his material give dignity and importance to these unassumingly modest pieces.

Clarissa Young Spencer, daughter of Brigham Young, writes in *One Who Was Valiant* of the wooden dolls of her youth (spent in Utah), "The heads were turned in our own carpenter shop," and "Betsy Long had a shop on Main Street where she made lovely wooden dolls."[24]

An unusual doll[25] is "Little Fanny," carved to include a child's dress of the 1880's. According to the story that has been handed down, she was made over two and one-half feet high to serve as a playmate for a little girl who had no sister.

A gentleman doll[26] was acquired in Maine. He is dressed in homespun but his fashionable hair suggests that around 1840, perhaps as a groom, he wore a more fashionable suit. The rounded cheeks, the well-modeled mouth and chin, suggest that the carver was a craftsman who had a routine way of carving heads; no amateur would work this way.

Another wooden doll[27] (Fig. 38), six inches high, from New Hampshire, is believed to be by a local carver from a Swiss settlement, and hence would probably date after 1850. It looks European; the fact that the figure is carved complete from head to foot suggests an origin in some locality where wood carving was indigenous. This again is the work of a competent artisan. It is significant that much emphasis is given to fully-rounded

FIG. 38. *Doll from New Hampshire.*

shapes and smooth surfaces, and that hands and feet are varied in position and not dwarfed, as is often the case in amateur work. The head is given no special emphasis, as if the type had existed well-formulated in the mind of the carver before he applied his knife to the wood. This carving depends on tradition and a skillful use of tools; it is impersonal and devoid of emotional content.

William Schimmel[28] (1817?–1890) was a Pennsylvania German folk artist and, according to tradition, a veteran of some war, Mexican, Civil or Franco-Prussian. A migratory worker, he went about the Pennsylvania countryside within a twenty-five-mile area from Carlisle to Newburg and from the Conodoguinet Creek to the North Mountain. Between farms and blacksmith shops he carved eagles (Fig. 39) in which the wings are attached separately. The one here illustrated has a spread of about two feet. Large and small roosters, parrots, squirrels, dogs, and a garden of Eden have also been attributed to Schimmel.

FIG. 39. *Eagle, attributed to Schimmel.*

His rough technique seems to reflect the character of the man. He had the reputation of having a temper, but the Pennsylvania Germans, to whom he belonged, understood and tolerated him. On one occasion, in 1880, he let his curses loose at the Cumberland County Fair, where he had exhibited but failed to receive a prize. On his death the Carlisle paper noted that "old Schimmel was apparently a man of a very surly disposition."[29] Today his carvings are in public and private collections.

Schimmel had a pupil in William Mountz, who carved eagles and other birds in a smoother style. We do not know how many other carvers there may have been in Pennsylvania, or whether there were any who worked along similar lines, but there are carvers living today who have adopted this style.

Small toys, Pennsylvania German in origin, form another category, continuing folk art models of German and Swiss tradition. Cavalrymen[30] on horseback in eighteenth-century uniforms, a wooden ship[31] on wheels with two masts and manned with wooden soldiers, sailors and a cannon; Noah's arks,[32] a toy carrousel[33] with three horsemen mounted on a small box and movable around a center pole, belong to these German- and Swiss-inspired types. The same is true of small carved and painted animals, like hens, roosters, squirrels, eagles, parrots and other birds. They[34] are called toys and sometimes linked to Schimmel. Little is known of makers and dates, except where the ownership within a family is on record.

Christmas putz[35] miniatures were made by George Huguenin (d. 1882). Though not a professional toy carver himself, he was descended from a toy-carving family of Travere, Switzerland. Huguenin, who was known as Higiny in his own region north of Stroudsburg in Newfoundland (formerly Hopedale), Pennsylvania, carved, about the middle of the nineteenth century, well-executed sheep, about two inches high. He painted them and covered them with genuine sheepskin pelts. He also carved barns, sheepfolds and stockades, houses and churches to go with the sheep, in which he was chiefly interested. The inspiration came from the toys Huguenin remembered and perhaps copied. Surviving imported sets with French and German labels suggest that such models were also available to him.

In chip-carving, small pieces are chipped or chiseled out, resulting in a uniform surface decoration. This technique demands more patience than skill. A wooden hen[36] of this type, seven inches high, is said to be from Cape Cod. The back of the bird, from head to tail, is one smooth curve without a break to suggest that birds, too, have bones and are not just inflated balloons. This tendency to minimize anatomical structure is universal with folk artists.

There is a type of amateur wood carving that specializes in little things, like "chains" and "balls-in-a-cage."[37] Wood carvers from Renaissance Florence to far-off China have delighted in carvings that surprise and mystify. Such carvers derive a childlike pleasure from a stunt that invariably causes the uninitiated to ask, "How did the ball get into the cage?" In this case the carver was an Alaskan fisherman.

Pipe heads and walking sticks also belong to this category of whittlers' creations. This pipe bowl[38] (Fig. 40) of Lincoln was done by a Minnesota carver of Scandinavian extraction. You can recognize Abraham Lincoln, but look at eye and cheek and you may agree, it is not quite human, more like ape than Abe. Judging from the sketch above, the front view is grim; perhaps this was unintentional on the part of the carver.

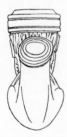

FIG. 40. *Pipe bowl, Head of Lincoln, c. 1860, by Sven Hassler from Marine, Minnesota.*

Among wooden toys we have some attractive horses attached to a thin board on wheels. Some are primitive, with cylindrical bodies, peg legs and sawed-out heads and necks, fitted together out of several pieces, or whittled with attached post-like legs.[39] Even in more sophisticated versions a basic simplicity reduces details to pleasantly abstract shapes.[40] In this type, the austere heads recall the slenderized shapes of early Greek art.

Home-made hobby horses were pieced together out of planks, varying in thickness and whittled to achieve a sense of three-dimensional bulk. Individual examples are attributed, by the owners, to the eighteenth century. Carving extends only to the separate portions; legs, head, neck and saddle. Their effect depends on an appeal of line and shape in the total structure. In these wood-carved horses folk art achieves a degree of abstraction that is timeless and is found the world over. Occasionally a rocking horse has a rhythmic curve of great vigor or a succession of soft undulating sweeps.[41] In others less ambitious, the effect is more static.[42] As the carver becomes more skillful and able to achieve greater realism, there may be a corresponding loss of vigor. The wood-carved horses of folk art thus repeat, in a short time-span, a development often met with through art history, but involving centuries.

A few isolated decorative carvings from Utah[43] seem to go back to an eighteenth-century German type of floral vases, called *Maikrüge*.[44] The German examples from Swabia (upper Danube region) are of the nineteenth century and are of painted tin. Like the maypole, such floral offerings go back to earlier heathen rites. Christianity sanctified pagan customs and used these artificial flowers as altar decorations. These carved wood decorations from Utah are about twenty inches high without the base. No longer naturalistic in the Swabian manner, they are highly stylized, unpainted and fitted into stone bases. Several variations are known to have been carved in 1899 by a man of the name of Malser. Floral decorations growing out of vases more like the German type are kept in the Basilica of Quebec, Canada.[45]

A group of canes, of which an example[46] was found in Michigan, shows the influence of the west in the choice of animals,

like fish and snakes that are carved in relief. Sometimes these
canes are traced to state prisons, and represent one form of
leisure-time activity. Though they carry the imprint of their
western environment, it is difficult to date them exactly. They
probably belong to the second half of the nineteenth century.

A head,[47] said to represent the head of a hanged man, has a
real distinction. It is owned by the Pony Express Museum at
Arcadia, California. It is from the California gold-rush days
and might be classed with works of migratory workers. It is an
unusual piece, unacademic and probably not by a professional
sculptor, and yet more sensitive than usually occurs in folk
carving. One wonders what oxbow incident might have inspired
the artist to carve his impressions with so much sympathy.

In the carvings of lumberjacks[48] we have folk art in its most
unsophisticated expression. Before the automobile, the lumberjacks of Wisconsin and Minnesota spent weekends in camp with
time on their hands. On some such occasion a group of Warring
Indians (Fig. 41) may have been created. Each horse and rider
is about four inches long; each is separate and movable. On first
sight, horses and men seem crude and ill-proportioned. Yet a
wholly negative appraisal overlooks the invention, the variation
in details and the liveliness of action. In spite of disproportion,
there is delicacy in the profiles and in the carving of bows and
arrows and in the elaboration of the feather headdress. We must
also admire the self-confidence of the carver, who could sur-
mount his lack of experience and carry the whole set through
to completion. Many a beginner would have been frustrated
when he found that his riders invariably came out too large.
There is real achievement here, in spite of an obvious lack of
training.

Decoys (Fig. 42) are imitation wild fowl; ducks, geese or
other birds, carved and painted to deceive the live birds and lure
them within range of the hunter's guns. Wooden decoys were
an improvement on those the Indians made of stuffed skins or
painted bulrushes. The carving of decoys was practiced in Colonial days, and reached its maturity about the time of the Civil
War. There were decoy makers[49] in New England, on Long
Island and along the Atlantic Coast down to the Gulf, and on
inland lakes. Decoys were made in quantities and specimens
are still available for collectors.

FIG. 41. *Warring Indians, carved by a lumberjack.*

FIG. 42. *Decoy, Blue-Winged Teal, from Milwaukee, Wisconsin, c. 1886. Made by Dr. Archer.*

Decoys are one form of wood carving that has continued down to the present day, in spite of competition from factory production. Decoys[50] are carved in the round, from a solid block of white pine or cedar. Another type[51] called "Stick-up" is flat, showing the profile, and is attached to a stick, so that it may be stuck in the grassy marshes where the birds come for seeds. The bodies are hewn out of the block and finished with the draw-knife and jackknife. The heads are made separately and at-tached; the eyes may be set in with glass or carved, but more often they are painted, like the rest of the body. Old decoys were painted in solid, flat colors.

There are other wooden birds that were carved by skilled craftsmen who were also naturalists. A dove (Fig. 43) belongs to this group. The sensitively felt shape shows a flowing con-tour with delicately rendered feathers and sturdy legs and claws. To give pleasure to the carver and to others was per-haps the main reason for spending so much effort on the perfec-tion of details.

FIG. 43. *Dove.*

Home-made wooden weathervanes were probably being produced during the whole of the last century, even though metal
was replacing wood and commercial metal vanes dominated the
field. The wooden weathervanes are typical of the unsophisticated, untrained amateur carver, and they make up a characteristic phase of American folk art. It was comparatively simple to
saw or chisel a flat wooden vane out of a board. It took more
skill and experience to make a vane that had depth.

A feathery bird[52] is the work of a professional, a carving by
Edbury Hatch. It should be seen from a moderate distance so
that the effect of the detail would not be lost. Weathervanes
often show some measure of realism, as here in the suggestion
of feathers. The legs, strong as posts, and the sturdy claws are
not photographically true to nature, but they are carved with a
vigor that indicates a superior craftsman. In the lowered head
and tail feathers there is an expression of vitality, and in the
firm contours, the simplified head, comb and beak, we sense the
artist who works with conviction. The liberties he takes with
nature are different from those taken by a less experienced
amateur.

The man who started with a flat board had to be satisfied with
a silhouette, but this limitation is no handicap for a weathervane that is to be seen from a distance. The bolder the contour,
the more effectively it stands out against the sky.

The cock for the church weathervane follows an old custom.
The attractive design is simple, direct and almost sophisticated.
The outline is nothing but two wiggles, with enough detail
added to suggest head and tail feathers. Such easy curves, at
best only a suggestion of a real bird, reflect a self-confident approach. One would hesitate to say that it was done by an amateur, for there is nothing of the tentative; it is completely self-
assured. The effect is also due to the tool used, a jigsaw. To an
extent, the tool can determine the design.

This horse weathervane (Fig. 44) has little to do with a real
horse, but it makes an effective silhouette. Its charm is in its
flowing contour, which is the carver's spontaneous expression,
uninfluenced by study or knowledge. This is a happy little animal, with a queer assortment of legs; some are angular, some

PLATE X. *Butcher's Sign, from Fairhaven, Massachusetts, 1835.*

FIG. 44. *Weathervane, horse, c. 1864–65, from Rocky Neck,*
*Gloucester, Massachusetts.*

soft and rubbery. He has a round, fiery eye and ears that stick
straight up. Running-horse weathervanes were often patterned
after Currier and Ives prints, but this one has no such professional look. What the folk artist on the amateur level has that
the academic artist sometimes lacks is a sense of freedom. He
combines this with a love of repetition, as in the parallel grooves
of mane and tail, which add interest through a contrast of tex-
tures. Here again is the ornamental character that we have
noted before.

This is one example of a home-made type of wooden weathervane that is found in variations. Each carver copied or adapted
as well as he could whatever was handy; no two are exactly
alike. At times the carver's way of simplifying his problem of
making a horse look like a horse produced surprising results. In
one example[53] the carver did not trouble himself with the difficult task of showing the hoofs of the horse. As a result of this

shortcut, the shape of the horse rises out of the base in a continuous flow of line that gives a pleasing unity to the silhouette. Another[54] shows the influence of a Currier and Ives print, or it may have been carved after a commercial metal vane which had copied the print. This same source is probably responsible for other wooden vanes[55] unless the wooden vane clearly antedates the commercial type.

Ornamentation based on a repetition of circles, squares, rectangles or merely lines gouged out of the wood is typical of folk art. Symmetry and simplification are more important than truth to nature, and decoration takes the place of scientific accuracy. The fish weathervane (Fig. 45) follows this well-established type of design, with a row of little blocks set along the upper and lower contours.

The same principle applied to the human figure is illustrated in the whirligig (Plate IX). A whirligig is a toy to be set up outdoors, so that the paddle-like arms, extending in opposite directions, are whirled around by the wind. The carving of this little fellow—he is but a foot in height—required only a minimum of skill. Representation has been reduced to abstraction; he is only a symbol of man. This whirligig goes by the name of Sailor Jack. Painted buttons may once have helped to emphasize his nautical character. One feels that objects such as this might have been turned out according to a pattern. They were probably made individually, as designs differ even where the type repeats.[56] This is folk art in the same way that European peasant art is folk art, repeating traditional patterns. Though the whirligig is presumably of the eighteenth century, such abstraction looks timeless.

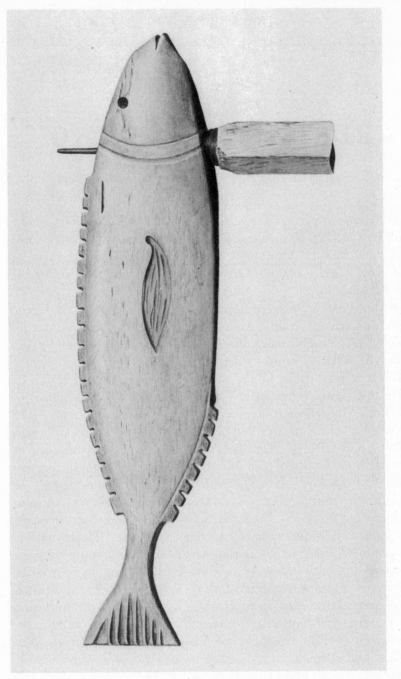

FIG. 45. *Weathervane, fish, c. 1888.*

# CHAPTER VI

# RELIGIOUS CARVING

The regions important for religious wood carving are those once held by Catholic France and Spain: Louisiana and New France and New Spain.[1] The states of Wisconsin, Illinois, Louisiana and New Mexico have left us wood-carved saints and statues of the Virgin.

A small carved wooden figure of St. Joseph,[2] now at St. Christopher's Convent in St. Louis, is from the former pioneer settlement of Kaskaskia, since the flood of 1881 submerged by the Mississippi River. From 1703 to 1765 this outpost, about seventy miles southeast of St. Louis, was the center of the fur trade. In style this figure reflects the French provincial of the School of Quebec. Monseigneur de Laval, first bishop of Quebec, had founded a school of arts and crafts in 1672 which in 1686 had thirty apprentices. Two schools of wood carvers grew up; one at Quebec and the other near Montreal. French masters,[3] like Le-Vasseur from Paris (1648), Leblond de Latour, master painter and carver from Bordeaux (1690),[4] the Baillairgés of four generations (1770–1850), François (1779–1782) and others brought the French Baroque style of carving to Canada.[5] These masters perpetuated the French Baroque influence and some of their descendants and followers produced in the region of the St. Lawrence River a simplified folk style of much charm. French missionaries traveled from Quebec to New Orleans founding settlements and baptizing Indians. A Canadian influence is reflected in various wood-carved Virgins and saints from Wisconsin and Illinois.

In this Virgin and Child (Fig. 46) from Wisconsin there is a

FIG. 46. *Virgin and Child from Sullivan, Wisconsin.*

Gothic element in the posture and in the backward tilt of the figure. But there is also the simplicity of folk art in the way the artist sees the contour, leaving the bulk of the figure intact. In these broad channels, in these drapery folds, stiff and unyielding, we feel the carver struggling with his material. We feel his determination in the uncompromising way one motif is placed beside another, the long strands of hair beside the curved drapery. It is this stressing of line and pattern that gives the ornamental effect.

A Virgin Mary[6] under three feet in height is carved out of a heavy plank over a foot wide, in the manner of a relief. The figure is said to have been the work of an Irish barber, John Bereman of Sullivan, Wisconsin.

A figure of St. Joseph (Fig. 47), about four feet high, inclines slightly backward, following the contour of the log. It came out of a board seven inches thick. If it were carved for a Roman Catholic church in Sullivan, Wisconsin, as reported, it could hardly be before 1850. The drapery tends to a symmetrical pattern which has only a general stylistic background. It might then point to an artisan who was isolated and dependent on

FIG. 47. *Saint Joseph, from Sullivan, Wisconsin.*

himself. But the figure as well as the Virgin Mary might be considerably earlier, before there were any permanent settlements in southern Wisconsin; if earlier one would think of a Canadian influence.

New Mexico also produced folk carvings during the nineteenth century. In this barren land of great distances, a style grew up that is unlike any other based on the European background.

It seems likely that there were but few midwestern wood carvings at a time when fur trading was the only occupation of the few settlers. In New Mexico every adobe hut had on its house altar a *santo*, like the Saint Raphael (Fig. 48). Many of them were destroyed before collectors became interested. These small statuettes were made by the religious image-makers, or *santeros*, who traveled with their santos from one village to another. The santos represented sacred persons on whom the natives depended for aid in sickness and for good crops at harvest time.

They were carved with a knife in soft pine or cottonwood, and painted upon a coating of gesso. Often only the upper part was of wood, the lower costume being of stiffened cloth secured by a wooden framework. Arms and any emblems held in the hands were carved separately. Hands are usually large and bodies slender. The earliest works were carved by the Spanish monks who were still familiar with the great works of seventeenth-century Spanish wood carving. But such influences that might have guided the first native wood carvers were absent during the later santeros period, 1750–1850, except for importations from Old Mexico. New Mexico was isolated geographically and culturally from the outside world. Left to themselves after about 1820, through repetition and modifications the santeros developed a degree of abstraction that strikes us today as original. These gaunt figures suggest an emotional intensity. The expression is largely in the contrast of the heads and huge hands with the emaciated bodies. The fact that they are highly ornamentalized makes them seem dramatic to modern eyes.

Though the santero was unschooled, his work was not that of a beginner; it has vigor and conviction. Some of the best examples are after 1820.

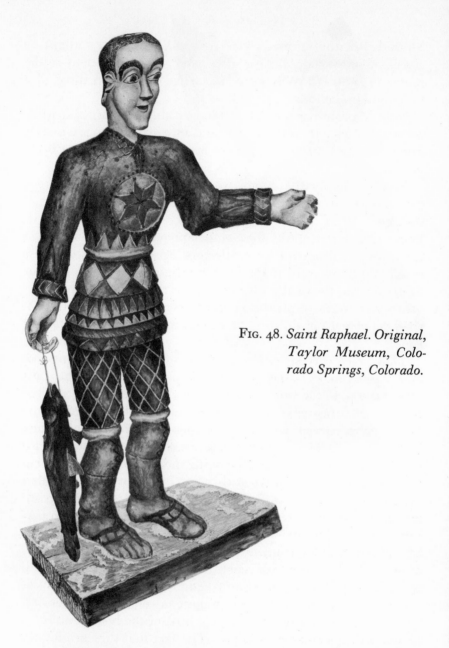

FIG. 48. *Saint Raphael. Original, Taylor Museum, Colorado Springs, Colorado.*

St. Joseph (Fig. 49) is the symbol of the ideal husband.[7] Young girls pray to him for a husband equally good. In the santos of New Mexico he holds the Christ Child in one hand and

PLATE XI. *Puppet "Judy." originally owned by puppeteer George Irving, c. 1870.*

PLATE XII. *Liberty, by Eliodoro Patete of Anawalt, West Virginia, after 1863.*

FIG. 49. *Saint Joseph (San Jose)*
*from New Mexico.*

often a lily in the other. This St. Joseph is in an indigenous New
Mexican tradition. The santero from New Mexico who carved
this figure worked in a region more isolated than Wisconsin. He
modified a tradition inherited from the early Franciscan fathers.
As native carvers took over, the style simplified without entirely
losing some of the original movement and gestures which characterized the types from which they descended. The child, a
little adult, holds up his hand in jubilation, as if the "glad tid-
ings" over the birth of the Savior had been projected onto the
child. Such gestures occur among the participants in medieval
altarpieces of Europe, and have survived in New Mexico as late
as the nineteenth century. Austerity and liveliness fuse in a
manner to produce a style which is only slightly differentiated
by personal idiosyncrasies.

Santiago or St. James (Fig. 50) is represented as the warrior

FIG. 50. *Santiago (on horseback).*

saint of Spain who battled against the Moors. The carver was
chiefly interested in making his santo important, so he mini-
mized the horse, which is merely an attribute. This piece has
been repaired several times, so that it is no longer attributed to
one santero; several have worked on it. In all its primitive simplicity, the concentration of the appeal on the head and on an
expansive gesture gives it an air of grandeur in spite of its small
size.

Since the bultos of New Mexico have been studied and compared, particularly during the last decade, attempts have been
made to separate them into groups with common characteristics,
making it plausible that each group might represent the work
of an individual.[8] One group, with Santa Cruz as point of origin,
tends to tall, lean figures. Other bultos, according to E. Boyd,
are by a santero, Miguel Aragon, and by an unidentified carver

who emphasized expression in the heads but slighted the body. A basic distinction has been made between a "classic santero type" with delicately carved features and hands and fine line ornamentation of garments and a more provincial type found in Mora and western San Miguel counties. In this type the features are consistently stylized and very similar, and some examples have fine black dots on eyebrows and lashes and small hoof-like feet with black shoes or boots.[9]

A group of nearly life-sized figures was related to the rites of the Penitente Brotherhood, the members of which re-enacted the Passion of Christ. Its central figure is Christ, the Man of Sorrows, bleeding from the wounds of the crucifixion. It is a devotional image created from several sources, to which the marks of the self-inflicted pain of the penitente have been added, all executed with blood-stained realism. The Easter performance of Holy Week, enacted by the Brotherhood as an act of penance, included the figure of Death with bow and arrow seated on a cart, as well as Christ crucified and entombed.

As New Mexico was opened up to commercial products after 1850, the native folk art was replaced by plaster figures. These looked more nearly like the great examples of European religious sculpture and were preferred to the home-made statues. The old bultos were now associated with a primitive culture that needed to be advanced to a higher, more civilized state. In one case, deliberate destruction added to the desire to be rid of the old figures. In one valley which was subject to violent storms, there was a belief that the burning of santos would help to avert disaster.[10]

Generally speaking, the carving of bultos came to an end in New Mexico as folk art had ceased to exist in backward regions of Europe. Wherever the railroad opened up out-of-the-way regions to the machine-made products of industry, there folk art lost its appeal. But not all creative wood carving ceased at the time the old manner was discouraged. In a letter from E. Boyd, Curator of the Museum of New Mexico, Palace of the Governors, a more encouraging aspect is described:

"There has always been a certain amount of creative work in New Mexico. However naive, it is original. Born in the second half of the nineteenth century, these late carvers continued the tradition to our own day. Among them were José Dolores Lopez, of Cordova, N. M., who died in 1942, and Celso Gallegos, of Agua Fria, six miles south of Santa Fé, who died in 1943."

Celso Gallegos is here illustrated by a figure of Saint George standing beside his horse above the dragon (Fig. 51). "He was a little gnarled man who worked mostly with a jackknife as his only tool, and he rarely added color to the native pine or cotton-wood which he carved. He considered himself a legitimate fol-lower of. the older santo makers. In his younger days he seems

Fig. 51. *Saint George and the Dragon by Celso Gallegos (d. 1943) at Agua Fria (Santa Fe).*

to have made many wooden slabs and crosses for the cemetery at Agua Fria. Few of these remain as the woods are so perishable when unprotected from the climate and no care is taken of them.

"After World War I, a Society for the Preservation of Spanish Colonial Arts was formed. One of its aims was to keep old crafts alive[11] among the Spanish people here. Thus Celso Gallegos, already past middle age, was encouraged to make not only santos and grave markers but various figures and reliefs of fanciful subjects, such as horses. His treatment of horses was very ap-pealing and free."

Probably the largest and most ambitious single piece of religious folk carving was made in Minnesota. It is the low relief carved wood altarpiece[12] in the Norwegian-American Historical Museum at Decorah, Iowa. Over twelve feet high and ten feet wide, it was done as late as 1890 by Lars Christensen (1839–1910), a Minnesota farmer from near Benson, who had emigrated from Norway. The carver was trained as a carpenter and blacksmith, but devoted his time to farming and carved in his spare time.

The lower right panel representing the Nativity with the shepherds (Fig. 52) is but a small part of the whole. The iconography of the twelve heads in the background is unusual. One would suspect that some recollections from the carver's village church in Norway might have determined his style, but that hypothesis does not seem to hold up under examination, except for the use of acanthus leaves. The design is probably the

FIG. 52. *Panel from Altarpiece; Nativity, carved by Lars Christensen, near Benson, Minnesota.*

carver's own creation; we need not assume that it is based on a model which he tried to emulate. As an experienced carver he had command of a repertory of shapes and by training before he left Norway in his twenty-fourth year he had acquired craftsmanship and technique. He treated the figure in the same decorative manner he used for border, panels and floral ornament, giving his design a basic unity of expression. An all-over decorative effect is here achieved which is unique in American folk art.

Where a more nearly European mode of living was perpetuated, there quality and craftsmanship came into their finest flowering. This produced, on the one hand, finely carved chests; on the other hand more homely cake molds. It would be futile to seek specifically American characteristics in a field where there was a common basis with European standards. Where a culture spreads, we expect a degree of continuity, which accounts for our finding among smaller home-made objects, examples which look as if they might have been imported.

Where activity toward practical ends was in evidence, there a native American trend unconsciously found expression. In shipbuilding, the effort went into the development of the vessel itself, culminating in the clipper ship; the figurehead became a by-product. Wood sculpture on a large scale served the purposes of commerce in an era of intense competition. To sell goods, not to exhibit art, was the immediate purpose of cigarstore Indians. Circus carvers, to whom speed and change were paramount, utilized whatever motifs were readily available and bent their efforts to attract a crowd to fill the big tent.

On a more individual level, the American temper shows itself in the variations with which carvers treated such subjects as weathervanes. These carvers were people who in a more settled community would have left artistry to professionals. Here is a case where lack of supply stimulated ingenuity, with the result that the amateur turned artist. A native element makes itself felt wherever necessity encourages the individual to discover his own power.

# NOTES

## CHAPTER I

1. Christensen, Erwin O.: The Index of American Design. New York, 1950, ch. 6, pp. 54–62.
Lipman, Jean: American Folk Art in Wood, Metal and Stone. New York, 1948, pp. 25–33. Figs. 4–24. *Scientific American*, August 7, 1909, p. 92; The Figurehead and its Story, quoting Baring-Gould: Strange Survivals and Superstitions.
Skerret, Robert G.: The Time-Honored Practice of Ornamenting Ships, in *The Rudder*, December 1919, p. 553.

2. Michel, André: *Histoire de l'Art.* Vol. VI, 2, p. 685.

3. Michel: *op. cit.*, p. 684.

4. Laughton, L. G. Carr: *Old Ship Figure-Heads and Sterns.* London, 1925, p. 14.

5. Laughton: *op. cit.*, p. 29.

6. Laughton: *op. cit.*, p. 20.

7. Pinckney, Pauline A.: *American Figureheads and Their Carvers.* 1940, p. 52.

8. Pinckney: (1940), p. 31.

9. Mass-Ca-131.

10. NYC-Ca-30.

11. Mass-Ca-40.

12. Mass-Ca-70.

13. Va-Ca-20.

14. Md-Ca-7.

15. Conn-Ca-3.

16. Marceau, Henri: *William Rush (1756–1883), The First Native American Sculptor.* Philadelphia, 1937. On the basis of a comparison with the bust of Captain Samuel Morris, carved in wood and signed Wm. Rush fecit, no. 20. See: File of Index correspondence, M. E. Hackney to Henri Marceau (1939) and subsequent MS on the Benjamin Franklin carved by William Rush by Malcolm Hackney.
About twenty wood carvings believed to be by Rush were collected by Henri Marceau for an exhibition at the Philadelphia Museum of Art (then named Pennsylvania Museum), 1937.
Pinckney, Pauline A.: (1940), pp. 85, 171.
*Antiques*, February 1941, p. 83.

17. In 1791 several painters and sculptors attempted to found, in Philadelphia, an art school which was to include drawing from a living model. This was more than public morals were able to endure, and the resulting controversy put an end to this plan. When the Pennsylvania Academy came into existence in 1805, plaster casts of famous statues like the Venus of Medici were exhibited. An admission fee of twenty-five cents was charged, and Monday was set aside for ladies exclusively.
Marceau: (1937), p. 16.

18. Pa-Ca-5B.
Hazard's Register of Pennsylvania, Vol. 8, 1931–32, p. 110.

19. Me-Ca-35.

20. William H. Tripp, Curator of the Whaling Museum of New Bedford, Massachusetts, where it is owned, attributes this figurehead to Charles A. L. Sampson. This figurehead, or one like it, is illustrated in *Arts and Decoration*, September 1932, p. 48, lower left, as having been at the time in a "Quebec garden."

21. Me-Ca-55.

22. Va-Ca-5.

23. R.I.-Ca-65. Ship *Aloha*, now dismantled, figurehead at Newport, Rhode Island Historical Society.

24. Me-Ca-39.

25. Me-Ca-74.
The 213 foot vessel was lost at sea June 30, 1897. Our knowledge of her figurehead is based on a photograph, from which the Index drawing was made.

26. Me-Ca-36.

27. Mass-Ca-74.

28. Mass-Ca-47.

29. Va-Ca-14.

30. NYC-Ca-158. The Belle of Oregon, carved by Charles Sampson, had a detachable arm. Now at the Webb Institute of Naval Architecture, Crescent Beach Road, Glen Cove, L. I., N. Y.

31. Va-Ca-6.

32. Mass-Ca-233.

33. Mass-Ca-14.

34. Mass Ca-3; Mass-Ca-88; Va-Ca-9;

Va-Ca-11; Va-Ca-12; Va-Ca-13; Me-Ca-66.

35. Mass-Ca-24; Mass-Ca-212; Mass-Ca-206; Conn-Ca-5; R I-Ca-173.

36. Mass-Ca-181.

37. Va-Ca-18.

38. Mich-Ca-80B.

39. Iowa-Mscl-36.

40. Bows of U.S.S. *Constitution* (Boston Navy Yard) and *Hartford* (Charleston Navy Yard). S C-Ca-4.
Bow from *Constellation* (1795). R I-Ca-59.
Billethead aboard *Constitution.*
Mass-Ca-115. Billethead, Peabody Museum, Salem, Massachusetts; Billethead, Nantucket Historical Association, and one at U.S. Naval Academy, Annapolis. *Antiques,* July 1936, p. 11, Fig. 3.
N. H.-Ca-37.

41. Mass-Ca-8.

42. Mass-Ca-53.

43. Va-Ca-30.

44. Me-Ca-23.

45. Va-Ca-26; S Cal-Ca-64.

46. Me-Ca-28; Conn-Ca-16.

47. La-Ca-7.

48. Mass-Ca-32.

49. Ill-Ca-53.

50. Pinckney: (1940), Ch. II, V.

51. *Harper's Weekly,* January 6, 1883, p. 13.

52. Va-Ca-17.

53. Stafford, Victor: John Haley Bellamy in *Antiques,* March 1935, pp. 102–110.
*Harper's Weekly,* January 6, 1883, p. 13.

54. Pinckney: (1940), List of Carvers, Appendix 3, pp. 186–203, gives over 700 names of carvers. Appendix 1 lists 144 Figureheads, Billets and Stern Carvings. The Index of American Design contains about 150, but only a small number duplicate those in the Pinckney list.

55. The following carvers are among those in this group: John Welsh (Boston); Sacred Cod (before 1769); State House, Boston.
Isaac Fowle (Boston): Figurehead of a Young Woman (c.1820). Old State House, Boston. Mass-Ca-9.
Laban S. Beecher (Boston): Andrew Jackson (1834). Marine Museum, New

York City NYC-Ca-6.
Joseph Verrill: (Rockland, Maine); Eagle (mid-nineteenth century). Privately owned. Me-Ca-60.
Woodbury Gerrish (Portsmouth, N.H.): Figurehead (1865). Privately owned. N.H.-Ca-5.
Charles A. L. Sampson (Bath, Maine): Figurehead for *Western Belle* of Bath (c. 1876). Peabody Museum, Salem, Massachusetts. Mass-Ca-57.
W. L. Seavey (Bangor, Maine): Ship's Carver Sign. Me-Ca-33.

56. Jenny Lind. Conn-Ca-31.
Commodore Perry. Mass-Ca-97.
Janus. Mass-Ca-131.
Rembrandt. Mass-Ca-108.
George Washington. Mass-Ca-140.
Indian Chief. Mass-Ca-40.
Marie Antoinette. Me-Ca-105.
Brooks Walker. Va-Ca-14, and others, not necessarily rendered in the Index.

57. The names of the vessels to which the figureheads belonged are known more often, but in by far the largest number of cases, there is no information available except as it is suggested by the figurehead itself.

58. Pinckney: (1940), Appendix 3, p. 186.

Between 1936 and 1942 the state projects of the Index of American Design prepared renderings of all kinds of wood carving, exclusive of architecture and furniture; California (northern), 38; (southern) 50; Colorado, 18; Connecticut, 54; Delaware, 22; Illinois, 73; Kansas, 13; Louisiana, 13; Maine, 106; Michigan, 113; Minnesota, 45; Missouri, 50; New Hampshire, 21; New Jersey, 15; New Mexico, 20; Ohio, 14; Pennsylvania, 62; Virginia, 31.
Christensen (1950), *op. cit.:* pp. 54–61.

### CHAPTER II

1. Mass-Ca-21; Little Admiral. Proceedings of the Bostonian Society, January 1917, p. 14.
Figure holding a pinch of snuff from Demuth's tobacco shop in Lancaster. Mass-Ca-134; Coachman.

2. Conn-Ca-4.

3. Mich-Ca-38 and Mich-Ca-40; in 1936 in the Waters Collection of Grand Rapids, Michigan.

4. Mass-Ca-2 and Christensen (1950), p. 62, fig. 117.

5. R.I.-Ca-178.

6. Pa-Ca-62. This figure once stood above Riggs Brothers, makers of Chronometers and Nautical Instruments in Philadelphia.

7. Index photo, no number.

8. Mass-Ca-152.

9. NYC-Ca-24; c. 1800. New York Historical Society.

10. Mass-Ca-120.

11. According to information given by Mr. Russel Leigh Jackson, Director.

12. La-Ca-6, now in the Louisiana State Museum in Baton Rouge.

13. NYC-Ca-129, now at the New York State Historical Association at Cooperstown.

14. 5,385 persons participated in the count. According to this, New York State reported 88; Pennsylvania, 60; Michigan, 59; Illinois, 52; Ohio, 36; Massachusetts, 32; Missouri, 28; Iowa, 27; California and Connecticut, 22 each; Maryland, 16; Wisconsin, 14; Indiana, 13; Virginia and Nebraska, 9 each; New Hampshire, 7; Kansas and Washington, 6 each; and so on down to 3, 2 and 1 per state. Canada reported 12. This census of wooden Indians indicated where the Indians stood or who owned them.

15. Shaw, Charles G.: *Antiques*, March 1934, p. 101ff. September 1939, pp. 131–133.

16. Morrison, J. L.: Passing of the Wooden Indian, *Scribner's Magazine*, October, 1928, p. 394.

Sanborn, Kate: *Hunting Indians in a Taxicab*, 1911, suggests but does not demonstrate that the solid wooden shop figures evolved out of painted boards carved in silhouette.

17. Morrison: *op. cit.*, pp. 395–396.

18. Sanborn: (1917), pp. 54–59.

19. Morrison: *op. cit.*, p. 396.

Weitenkampf, Frank: Lo, the Wooden Indian, in *New York Times*, August 3, 1890, p. 13: The name of the first man to introduce carved figures as tobacco signs in New York was Chicester, carver between 1850–1860. To date, Morrison, Sanborn and Weitenkampf have furnished background information on cigar-store figures.

20. Various dealers are known, like Edward Hen, Thomas W. Brooks of New York and Chicago (1848–1860); James A. Brooks (1890–1902); Samuel Robb; Isaac Lewis of New York; William Demuth, Julian Theodore Melchers, Herman Matzen, Theodore Crongeyer of Detroit; Fritz Decker of Philadelphia; John P. Yaegerarn and Pierre Caspari of Baltimore.

21. Morrison: *op. cit.*, p. 396.

22. *Tobacco*, including *The Tobacco News*, an Illustrated Journal. New York, April 8, 1887, p. 2. The Tobacconist's Sign.

23. Morrison: *op. cit.*, p. 396.

24. Weitenkampf: *op. cit.*, and *Magazine of Art*, December 1940, mentions several carvers and gives the figures they carved, like Thomas White in S.A. Robb's shop (Sullivan in Baseball Suit); Charles Dowler of Providence, Rhode Island (Dude) and others.

25. *Tobacco, op. cit.*, p. 2.

26. *Harper's Weekly*, January 6, 1883, p. 13.

27. Morrison: *op. cit.*, p. 404.

28. Morrison: *op. cit.*, p. 23.

29. Weitenkampf: *op. cit.*

30. Krieger, Herbert W.: *American Indian Costumes* in U.S. Museum Annual Report, 1928.

31. Sanborn: (1911), p. 67–68. In about 1875 he (Francis Dreves, Baltimore dealer in cigar-store figures) commissioned a German sculptor from Munich to carve two very fine Indians at a cost of $115.00 each.

32. Me-Ca-98.

33. This particular statue, the Augustus of Prima Porta in the Vatican, was discovered in 1863, so that the cigar-store Indian must be of a subsequent date.

Morrison, *op. cit.*, p. 404, writes: "The sculptors originated designs or copied book illustrations or prints."

34. *Tobacco, op. cit.*, p. 2.

35. Morrison: *op. cit.*, p. 403.

36. *Washington Evening Star*, August 21, 1932. "Herman Kruske, about 1842 carved Sitting Bull for Bob Parsons, pioneer tobacco dealer of Ashland, Wisconsin."

37. Minn-Ca-41; Mich-Ca-41.

38. CHIEFS: Kan-Ca-5; Ill-Ca-27; Mass-Ca-66 Sturbridge Village; Mo-Ca-17; Mo-Ca-7; Mass-Ca-232; Pa-Ca-11; Pa-

Ca-27 Philadelphia Museum of Art; Pa-Ca-7d Bucks County Historical Museum, Doylestown, Pennsylvania; R.I.-Ca-12 and R.I.-Ca-13, King Philip Museum. R.I.-Ca-23; R.I.-Ca-18; R.I.-Ca-34c, 1890. R.I.-Ca-54c, 1890. Me-Ca-15; Me-Ca-21; Me-Ca-30. Minn-Ca-40 from Wisconsin, c. 1880. Mich-Ca-28; Mich-Ca-19; Mich-Ca-20; Mich-Ca-56, Edison Institute, Dearborn, Michigan; Mich-Ca-74, attributed to Julius Melcher, c. 1875; SoCal-52; SoCal-58(a); SoCal-Ca-94a; Cal-Ca-292.

POCAHONTASES: Ill-Ca-14; Iowa-Mscl-89; Mass-Ca-51; and Mass-Ca-30; Old Sturbridge Village; Mass-Ca-62; Me-Ca-30; Me-Ca-15; Samuel A. Robb, 114 Center Street, New York City, signed. Mich-Ca-6; Mich-Ca-42; Mich-Ca-31; Mich-Ca-29; Mich-Ca-35; Mich-Ca-26; Mich-Ca-53 and Mich-Ca-61, two renderings, Edison Institute, Dearborn, Michigan. Mich-Ca-21; Mich-Ca-20; Mich-Ca-25B. Mo-Ca-3; NYC-Ca-17, Historical Society, NYC. R.I.-Ca-20, King Philip Museum, Bristol, R.I.

39. CHIEFS: Iowa-Mscl-102; Iowa-Mscl-90; Mo-Ca-4, made in Alton, Ill.; Mo-Ca-5. NYC-Ca-31; Mich-Ca-11.

POCAHONTASES: Mass-Ca-87, 2½ feet high; Mich-Ca-5, Mich-Ca-33, Hopi Boy. NYC-Ca-31.

40. CHIEFS: R.I.-Ca-15; N.H.-Ca-168; N.H.-Ca-57; Iowa-Mscl-95; Ill-Ca-13; Conn-Ca-53; Pa-Ca-9; Mich-Ca-11; Mich-Ca-59; Me-Ca-17; La-Ca-4; Mich-Ca-10; Mich-Ca-24; Mich-Ca-62; Mich-Ca-7; Mich-Ca-36; Mich-Ca-18.

POCAHONTASES: Mich-Ca-4; R.I.-Ca-26; Me-Ca-16; SoCal-Ca-88; Mich-Ca-6; N.H.-Ca-1; Mich-Ca-81; Mich-Ca-60; Me-Ca-107.

41. CHIEFS: R.I.-Ca-16; R.I.-Ca-27, King Philip Museum, Bristol, R.I.; Iowa-Mscl-104, 1883, Chicago; Wis-Mscl-38; Ohio-Ca-17; Iowa-Mscl-96, c. 1870, Decorah, Iowa, Norwegian-American Museum.

POCAHONTASES: NYC-Ca-43; Mich-Ca-30; Mich-Ca-102; Va-Ca-23; Mich-Ca-14; N.H.-Ca-7; Mich-Ca-96; N.H.-Ca-3; N.H.-Ca-2; R.I.-Ca-160, King Philip Museum, Bristol, R.I.; Md-Ca-5; Md-Ca-6; Pa-Ca-10.

42. CHIEFS: Mich-Ca-18; Mich-Ca-32; Mich-Ca-34; Mich-Ca-5; Mich-Ca-87;

Iowa-Mscl-80; Mass-Ca-101; Minn-Ca-30; Md-Ca-4; Cal-Ca-277.

POCAHONTASES: Mich-Ca-9; R.I.-Ca-190; R.I.-Ca-16, King Philip Museum, Bristol, R.I.; So.Cal-63, Pony Express Museum, Arcadia, California.

43. CHIEFS: Pa-Ca-29; Mich-Ca-58; Mo-Ca-8; Minn-Ca-24.

POCAHONTASES: Ariz-Ca-38, Heard Museum, Phoenix, Arizona. c. 1875(?).

44. Me-Ca-98.

45. Me-Ca-20.

46. SoCal-Ca-61.

47. Cal-Ca-299.

48. Mich-Ca-32.

49. Md-Ca-8.

50. R.I.-Ca-61.

51. Lipman: (1948), pp. 105–116. Whitehill, Virginia A.: American Circus Carving in *Magazine of Art*, May, 1943, p. 172. Howe, Florence Thompson: Carved Wood Circus Wagon Figures, in *Antiques*, August 1947, p. 120. Christensen: (1950), pp. 152–159. Carvers of figureheads and shop figures are also mentioned as circus carvers, as S.A. Robb (1874) in New York City and Thomas W. Brooks (1881–1882) in Chicago. Names of circus wagon builders have also been collected. Research File, Index of American Design.

52. Conn-Ca-51.

53. Conn-Ca-23B.

54. R.I.-Ca-189.

55. As told the author by Mr. William Warren of Litchfield, Connecticut.

56. Jones, Barbara: *The Unsophisticated Arts* (England, 1951), pp. 29–36. Carrington, Noel and Hutton, Clarke: *Popular English Art* (England, 1945).

57. Mo-Ca-9; Mo-Ca-15; Mo-Ca-17; Mo-Ca-18; Mo-Ca-21; Mo-Ca-24; Mo-Ca-29; Mo-Ca-30; Mo-Ca-33; Mo-Ca-36, 37; Mo-Ca-43, 44; Mo-Ca-50, according to Mr. Lawrence Sickman, Sophian Plaza, Kansas City, Missouri; Kan-Ca-1, according to Paul D. Parker of Leavenworth, Kansas.

58. Circus animals attributed to Charles Louff according to a report from the Island Park Amusement Company of Riverton, Rhode Island, are: Horses, R.I.-Ca-136; R.I.-Ca-68. Goat, R.I.-Ca-79; Dog, R.I.-Ca-80. A pair of tigers, R.I.-Ca-67. A reindeer and a rabbit,

R.I.-Ca-130, R.I.-Ca-142 may also be his.
59. R.I.-Ca-79.
60. R.I.-Ca-130.
61. R.I.-Ca-80.
62. Mass-Ca-205; R.I.-Ca-131; R.I.-Ca-129.
63. Mass-Ca-194.
64. Jones: (England, 1951), pp. 24, 27.
65. R.I.-Ca-181.
66. R.I.-Ca-158.
67. The Index has recorded several sets of different owners.
68. Mich-Mscl-98 is believed to be of about 1785. Wooden body and wooden hands made in Italy.
69. The Punch and Judy set has 21 figures.
70. Index Record Files.
71. Mich-Mscl-68.
72. Mich-Mscl-15, Diefendorfer; Mich-Mscl-4, Lano.
73. Cal-Mscl-352; Cal-Mscl-298; Cal-Mscl-299; Cal-Mscl-131; Cal-Mscl-327.

CHAPTER III

1. Kimball, Fiske: *Mr. Samuel McIntire, Carver, the Architect of Salem.* 1940.
Dyer, Walter A.: *Early American Craftsmen.* 1915, pp. 16–40.
2. Keyes, Homer Eaton, in *Antiques,* January 1932, p. 12; April 1933, p. 142, Fig. 2.
Other portraits by McIntire: (1) a carved wood profile in the Essex Institute, Salem, after Wright's Etching (1790). Fiske Kimball in *Antiques, op. cit.,* January 1930, p. 39, Figs. 8 and 9 (2) Bust of Voltaire, in The American Antiquarian Society, Worcester, Massachusetts. Homer Eaton Keyes in *Antiques,* October 1935, p. 139.
3. Bentley, William: *The Diary of William Bentley,* 1905–14. Vol. 2, pp. 328, 452. William Bentley, pastor of the East Church of Salem and a contemporary of McIntire, characterized him in his Diary, May 21, 1798, and October 8, 1802, by noting: "I cannot say that he (McIntire) has expressed anything in the bust which agrees with the Governor. . . . He cuts smoother than Skillin, but he has not his genius."
4. Kimball (1940): p. 139, Fig. 363; also *Antiques,* The Editor's Attic, October 1935, p. 139.

Mass-Ca-55.
5. Kimball (1940): p. 139, Fig. 363. Also *Antiques,* January 1930, Figs. 8 and 9.
6. Kimball (1940): p. 138, Figs. 360, 361.
7. La-Ca-10.
8. Bishop, Julia Truitt in *The Times-Democrat,* February 9, 1913, p. 25.
9. NYC-Ca-70.
10. R.I.-Ca-97. Dates and information by letter from Herbert O. Brigham, Librarian, Newport Historical Society.
11. Mass-Ca-98.
12. Eisen, Gustavus A.: *Portraits of Washington,* c. 1932. Vol. III, p. 858; Fig. CCXLI, p. 949.
13. Minn-Ca-33.
14. Miller, Dorothy: *The Life and Work of David G. Blythe,* p. 15.
Gardner, Albert Ten Eyck: *Yankee Stone Cutters,* 1945, p. 6off.
*Biographical Dictionary* mentions wood carving in the biographies of nine out of over one hundred sculptors born between 1800 and 1830; some are in addition to those mentioned in the Pinckney list. Some forty or fifty life-size wooden statues, including Washington, Adams, Jefferson, Lord Nelson, once embellished the grounds of the Lord Dexter mansion at Newburyport. One statue (William Pitt) and fragments exist in private possession. *Antiques,* March 1923, pp. 107–108; August 1945, p. 78.
Howells, John Mead: *The Architectural Heritage of the Merrimack,* 1941, pp. 77–79; Figs. 83–85; p. 81, Fig. 87.
Jones, Louis C.: *The Folk Art Collection,* in *Art in America,* April 1950, pp. 109–123.
15. Md-Ca-9.
16. Pa-Ca-30.
17. Del-Ca-6.
18. R.I.-Ca-73.
Other wood-carved portraits are discussed and illustrated in *American Folk Art* (1948) by Jean Lipman, pp. 176–178 and Figs. 178–183.
19. Christensen: (1950), p. 193, Fig. 376.
20. Christensen: (1950), p. 70, Fig. 35.
21. Swan, Mabel M.: *Antiques,* December 1931, p. 342, Fig. 8; March, 1948, p. 198, Fig. 1.

The Skillin family has been investigated by Leroy L. Twing in two reports: The Ancestors of John and Simeon Skillin, Carvers, 1777–1806, and The Four Skillins. Research File, Index of American Design.

In 1873 Samuel Adams Drake in his *Old Landmarks of Boston* attributed a statue of Mercury to Simeon Skillin. In 1887 Edward G. Porter, author of *Rambles in Old Boston*, called Simeon the "ablest wood carver of his time." Porter reports as follows: "Most of the figureheads that issued from the port of Boston for many years were made by Mr. Skillin. Such was his genius that he might be called an artist rather than an artisan." On John Skillin's death, January 24, 1800, the following comment appeared in his obituary in the *Chronicle:* "He was for many years the most eminent of his profession."

22. The identification of works by the Skillins is based on the discoveries of documents by Mabel M. Swan as reported in *Antiques* of December 1931.

A signed work by "S. Skillin, Boston 1793" is a wooden figure. See *Antiques*, July 1936. Though perhaps less obviously comparable to these two figures of Justice and Hope, this figure shows a bowknot on the ribbon around the waist. This same motif occurs on the central figure of the Garvan chest-on-chest (Yale) and on one figure of the Bolles secretary (Metropolitan) and on the two figures of Hope and Justice. S. A. Drake (*Old Landmarks of Boston*) and Bacon (*Dictionary of Boston, 1886*) agree that two wooden figures, Hope and Justice, ornamented the front of the second Boston Customs House located on the north side of State Street. In 1810 the first building designed for a customs house was erected in Custom House Street. (Report from Lois Shoemaker, Boston Public Library, to the author, March 22, 1949). This indicates that the figures seen by Drake and Bacon must have been in existence at least as early as 1810. This Justice may be compared with Tragedy, one of two figures carved by Rush for the Chestnut Street Theater in Philadelphia. Rush is the academic mannerist, who derives from the Italian Baroque; his style is chilly and over-

wrought. Marceau, (1937), **Fig. 3**.

23. Christensen: (1950), p. 193, Fig. 376.

Christensen: *Antiques,* January 1950.

24. For this attribution Mabel Swan in 1931 prepared the ground, in an article in *Antiques*, reporting on a bill she found in the records of the Derby family of Salem, rendered by John and Simeon Skillin in 1793 for four Garden Figures.

25. Compare another wood figure, Hope, twenty-two inches high, at the Essex Institute in Salem, Massachusetts, attributed to Simeon Skillin. *Antiques*, October 1935, p. 140, Fig. 2. Mass-Ca-41.

John Fisher's Justice, Pa-Ca-12A.

26. Ohio-Ca-13. The Journal of the Cincinnati Society of Natural History. Vol. XXII, no. 4, April, 1945, p. 12. Note on Powers' carved wood figure on a column, "somewhere on Second Street Cincinnati in 1851." *Cincinnati Times Star*, April 25, 1940, in article by Henry L. Fry.

27. R.I.-Ca-32.

28. Mass-Ca-18.

29. R.I.-Ca-112.

30. Mass-Ca-76.

31. R.I.-Ca-179. King Philip Museum, Mount Hope, Bristol, R.I. According to the *Courier-Journal* of Louisville, Kentucky, March 12, 1952, and reports by Miss Harriet Adams, former Director of Junior Art Gallery of the Louisville Free Public Library, and Mr. Donald H. MacLean who rescued and now owns the statue.

CHAPTER IV

1. Allen, Edward B.: Early American Carving in *International Studio*, May 1924, p. 95.

2. Howells, John Mead: *The Architectural Heritage of the Piscataqua*, 1937, Figs. 26, 27.

3. Vaughan, Dorothy M.: Governor Langdon Memorial Mansion of Portsmouth, New Hampshire, in *Old Time New England*. Vol. XXXIX, no. 1, July 1948.

4. Kimball, Fiske: *Domestic Architecture of the American Colonies and the Early Republic*, 1927. Figs. 94, 95; pp. 126–127.

5. Cornelius, Charles O.: Some Early American Doorways in *Bulletin* of the

Metropolitan Museum of Art. October, 1927, pp. 239–247.

6. Waterman, Thomas T.: *The Dwellings of Colonial America*, 1950. pp. 63 (Kenmore); 85 (Brenton); 103 (Brice); 105 (Harwood); 165 (Powel, Blackwell); 181 (Whitby Hall); 228 (Philipse Manor); 269, (The Lindens).

7. Allen (1924): *op. cit.*, p. 93.

8. Kimball (1927): *op. cit.*, Figs. 100–101; pp. 132–133.

9. Kimball (1940): Figs. 5, 89–92; 92–202.

Chamberlain, Samuel: *Salem Interiors*, 1950, pp. 100, 101, 109, 115, 125, 127, 147, 161.

10. Kimball (1940): pp. 47–48.

11. Kimball (1940): Figs. 9, 15, 150, 200, 249–250; 217–218; 340, 342–347, 366–373.

12. Letter of Mrs. A. J. Barker.

13. Photograph I.A.D. Letter of E. Milby Burton, Director.

14. Me-Ca-27.

15. Me-Ca-1; Me-Ca-4.

16. Mass-Ca-231; Mass-Ca-81; Mass-Ca-82, by W. H. Rumney, replacing the Colonial "Lion and Unicorn" destroyed by patriots in 1776.

17. Hatch wood carvings, Me-Ca-78–Me-Ca-89.

18. *Art in America*, 1600–1865 (Radio Broadcast Illustrated Guide), 1934, Chicago University Press, p. 39.

19. *American Heritage* 1948. Denver Art Museum Exhibition Catalog, p. 14.

20. *Art in America* 1934, p. 40.

21. R.I.-Ca-119.

22. Cal-Ca-14.

23. Cal-Ca-18; Cal-Ca-15; Cal-Ca-59; Cal-Ca-51.

24. Metropolitan: NYC-Fu-384. H. 7″, L. 23″, W. 16½″. Oak.
NYC-Fu-235. H. 9½″, L. 28″, W. 19″. Oak and Pine. Initials. H.S.
Brooklyn: NYC-Fu-392; NYC-Fu-27. Date 1686 carved on box; pine with front of oak, L. 32½″, W. 19″, H. 8¼″.
Boston: Mass-Fu-66. Oak. L. 27½″.
Mass-Fu-64. Oak with pine bottom. L. 21¾″.

25. Lockwood (1926): Vol. I, p. 379, Fig. L.
Christensen (1950): p. 123, Fig. 239.

26. Lockwood (1926): Vol. I, p. 23.

27. Lockwood (1926): Vol. I, p. 25, Fig.

8. Bolles Collection, Metropolitan Museum. Lyons, I. P.: The Oak Furniture of Ipswich, Massachusetts. *Antiques*, November and December 1927, Vol. 32. NYC-Fu-352.
Another chest from Guilford, Connecticut. Conn-Fu-1. New Haven Colonial Historical Society.

28. Lockwood (1926): Vol. I, pp. 23, 28. Fig. 13 and the same NYC-Fu-295.

29. Lockwood (1926): Vol. I, p. 336. Fig. I. Another attributed to Disbrowe, NYC-Fu-240, original Metropolitan Museum.

30. Conn-Fu-41.

31. Lockwood (1926): Vol. I, p. 39. Fig. 27. Conn-Fu-25A.
Luther, C. F.: The Hadley Chest. In *Antiques*, October 1928, pp. 338–340.

32. Lockwood (1926): Vol. I, p. 341. Fig. VIII.

33. Lockwood (1926): Vol. I, p. 343.

34. Nutting, Wallace: Carved Spoon Racks. In *Antiques*, June 1925, pp. 312–315.

35. Sack, Albert: Fine Points of Furniture, Early American, 1950. p. 12.

36. Sack (1950): pp. 16, 17.

37. Sack (1950): pp. 30–38.

38. Hipkiss, Edwin J.: *Eighteenth Century American Art*. The M. and M. Karolik Collection. 1941. p. 148, Fig. 85; p. 152, Fig. 89.
Sack (1950): p. 40.

39. Christensen (1950): p. 131. Fig. 256.

40. Lockwood (1926): Vol. I, p. 106. NYC-Fu-353.

41. Downs, Joseph: Metropolitan Museum of Art *Bulletin*. December 1932. NYC-Fu-121, Highboy; NYC-Fu-323, Lowboy.
Lockwood (1926): Vol. I, p. 109.

42. Downs, Joseph: Metropolitan Museum of Art *Bulletin*, December 1918.

43. Hipkiss (1941): pp. 100–102, Figs. 54, 55.

44. *Antiques*, April, 1932. Fig. on p. 160, Secretary on loan to the Monmouth County Historical Society, Freehold, New Jersey.

45. Kimball, Fiske: Furniture Carvings by Samuel McIntire, in *Antiques*, February, 1931, pp. 117–119.

46. Sack (1950): pp. 54–55.

47. Sack (1950): p. 152, and NYC-Fu-s11, Metropolitan Museum.

48. Cornelius, Charles O.: The Distinctiveness of Duncan Phyfe, in *Antiques*, November 1922, pp. 204–208. Fig. 2.
49. Del-Fu-104.
50. Hipkiss (1941): p. 202, No. 135; p. 204, no. 136; p. 206, no. 137. Sack (1950): p. 209 (right).
51. Brown, Mary Louise: John Welch, Carver. In *Antiques*, January 1926, pp. 28–30; Figs. 1 and 3.
52. Downs, Joseph: *American Furniture, Queen Anne and Chippendale Periods* 1952, no. 137.
53. *op. cit.*, no. 170.
54. *op. cit.*, no. 197.
55. NYC-Mscl-104; Wis-Fu-10; NYC-Vic-13; Iowa-Fu-49; NYC-Ca-56; NYC-Mscl-92; Utah-Mscl-25; Fla-Ca-2; La-Fu-1; SoCal-Fu-95(a); Del-Fu-67.
56. Ohio-Ca-12.
57. SoCal-Fu-92.
58. SoCal-Fu-64(a).
59. Christensen (1950): p. 39, Fig. 70.
60. Christensen (1950): p. 38, Fig. 66.
61. SoCal-Ca-3(b).
62. SoCal-Ca-7(a).
63. SoCal-Ca-3(a); SoCal-Ca-31(l) (j) (c). Santa Ines Mission, dedicated 1817.
64. SoCal-Ca-72. Santa Barbara Mission c. 1820.
65. SoCal-Fu-106(a).
66. SoCal-Fu-110(b).
67. SoCal-Fu-112(b).
68. SoCal-Ca-14(a).
69. Plath, Iona: *The Decorative Arts of Sweden*, New York, 1948. p. 145. Wis-Fu-3.

CHAPTER V

1. Christensen (1950): Ch. 13, pp. 135–142.
2. Pine Sea-chest. NYC-Fu-400. Christensen (1950): p. 41, Fig. 73.
3. Adams, Ruth: *Pennsylvania Dutch Art* 1950. The American Arts Library. Stoudt, John Joseph: *Pennsylvania Folk Art, An Interpretation*, 1948. Hynson, Garret, and Nash, Susan Higginson: Design in Yankee Butter Molds, in *Antiques*, Feb. 1942, pp. 131–133. Larsen, Peter: Butter Stamps and Molds, in *Antiques*, July 1939, pp. 29–30. Lichten, Frances: *Folk Art of Rural Pennsylvania*, 1946, pp. 117–121.
4. Hynson and Nash: *op. cit.*, p. 131.
5. Recollection of E. H. Jones of the Department of Agriculture, Montpelier, Vermont. March, 1939. Research File, Index of American Design.
6. Hynson and Nash: *op. cit.*, pp. 131–133.
7. Pa-Mscl-109.
8. Pa-Mscl-322.
9. Mich-Ca-110.
10. NYC-Ca-51. Drepperd, Carl W. in *Antiques*, November 1941, p. 281.
11. NYC-Ca-49.
12. NYC-Ca-50B.
13. R.I.-Ca-171.
14. Knittle, Rhea Mansfield: Early Decorative Arts in Ohio, in *Antiques*, January 1946, p. 32.
15. Mo-Ca-49. Ohio-Ca-19. Information handed down in the family; name carved in edge of mold carved on both sides.
16. Christensen (1950): Ch. 14, pp. 143–151.
17. Pa-Mscl-43.
18. N.J.-Toys-32.
19. Va-Mscl-3.
20. Mich-Mscl-93; La-Mscl-2; NYC-Toys-95; NYC-Toys-97.
21. SoCal-Ca-41.
22. St. George, Eleanor: *Dolls of Three Centuries*, 1951, p. 103.
23. Mich-Ca-89.
24. Dolls in the Utah Desert. In *Hobbies*, December 1940, p. 21.
25. Ill-Ca-40.
26. Ohio-Ca-10.
27. R.I.-Ca-114.
28. Flower, Milton E.: Schimmel the Woodcarver, in *Antiques*, May-October, 1943, p. 164ff.
29. Flower: *op. cit.*, p. 166. Christensen (1950): p. 135, no. 267.
30. Pa-Ca-48 and Karlinger, Hans: *Deutsche Volkskunst*, 1938. p. 199.
31. Pa-Ca-23 and Karlinger, (1938) p. 196 from Berchtesgaden.
32. Mich-Mscl-47. Robacker, Earl F.: Pennsylvania German Wood Carvings. In *Antiques*. June 1946. p. 369.
33. NYC-Mscl-Toys-47, and Karlinger, (1938), p. 197.
34. Mass-Ca-35, Rooster, Pheasant, Parrot. Mass-Ca-46, Parrots. Del-Ca-19, Bird; NYC-Ca-166, Parrot; NYC-Ca-1, Rooster; NYC-Ca-175, Rooster from Freehold, New Jersey; NYC-Ca-159, Squirrel; NYC-Ca-169, Squirrel.

35. Robacker, Earl F.: *op. cit.*, pp. 369–371.

36. Me-Ca-72.

37. Wash-Ca-4.

38. Minn-Ca-5.

39. NYC-Ca-189.

40. Pa-Ca-63.

41. Mass-Ca-180; NYC-Mscl-Toys-58;

42. Mich-Mscl-121.

43. Utah-Mscl-95; Utah-Mscl-94; Utah-Mscl-86.

44. Karlinger, Hans: (1938), p. 227.

45. Barbeau, Marius: *The Arts of French Canada, 1613–1870*. 1946. Loan Exhibition catalog, Plate VIII, Figs. 34a and 34b.

46. Mich-Ca-67.

47. Christensen (1950): p. 138, Fig. 272.

48. Iowa-Ca-4.

49. Barber, Joel: *Wild Life Decoys* 1934.
Lipman: (1948), pp. 131-135.

50. NYC-Ca-132 (Mallard); R.I.-Ca-170 (Mallard); Cal-Ca-308 (Teal); Wis-Ca-7.

51. NYC-Ca-145; Ill-Ca-50; NYC-Ca-131; NYC-Ca-207.

52. Me-Ca-87. (carved); R.I.-Ca-157 (sawed).

53. NYC-Ca-151.

54. Mass-Ca-220.

55. NYC-Ca-155; Mass-Ca-72; NYC-Ca-148.

56. Mass-Ca-271; Mass-Ca-106; NYC-Ca-197.

CHAPTER VI

1. Wilder, Mitchell, A., and Breitenbach, Edgar: *Santos, The Religious Folk Art of New Mexico* 1943.
Boyd, E.: *Saints and Saint Makers of New Mexico* 1946.
Houghland, Willard, and Bear, Donald: *Santos, A Primitive American Art.* Collection of Jan Kleijkamp and Ellis Monroe, New York 1946.
Barbeau, Marius: *The Arts of French Canada, 1613–1870*, 1946.
Christensen (1950): Ch. 2, p. 24; Ch. 3, pp. 28–40.

2. Belting, Natalia Marce: Vanished Kaskaskia, in *Antiques.* November 1941. pp. 282–284, Fig. 1.

3. Barbeau (1946), p. 21.

4. Richardson, E. P., and Grigant, Paul L.: *The French in America, 1520–1880.* Catalog, Detroit Institute of Arts, 1951.

5. Barbeau (1946, Plate X, Figs. 48, 49, 54.

6. Ill-Ca-38.

7. Halseth, Odd S.: "Saints of the New World," in *International Studio*, September 1929, p. 32.

8. Wilder and Breitenbach (1943), Plates 26, 27, 30, 33, 34.
Boyd (1946): pp. 59–68.
Christensen (1950): p. 13, Fig. 61; p. 34, Fig. 62.

9. Boyd, in a detailed report to the author differentiates between the types of New Mexican bultos.

10 Houghland and Bear (1946): p. 10.

11. Efforts to keep the folk arts alive as an economic measure to assist people to add to their incomes are noteworthy in the Southern Highlands and in New England. The Russell Sage Foundation and other agencies, private and state-supported, have been active in this field. See Eaton, Allen H.: *Handicrafts of the Southern Highlands*, 1937, Ch. XI. Whittling and Carving in Wood, pp. 179–186. Also *Handicrafts of New England*, 1949, Ch. X, Carving and Whittling, pp. 168–188.

12. Christensen (1950): p. 24, Fig. 44.

# EARLY AMERICAN WOOD CARVING
## IN ART MUSEUMS AND HISTORICAL SOCIETIES

### A PARTIAL LIST

*This list is a sampling from various public museums in different parts of the country; no comprehensive survey was intended. There are no doubt wood carvings in other public institutions and in many private collections. It is hoped that this list will call attention to places where wood carving may be found for appreciation and study, and thereby add to a growing interest in American crafts and folk arts.*

*Colorado.* DENVER ART MUSEUM.
Estimated total, 20, including a fine large Christ on the Cross, an Indian type Christo from the Morado at Mora; a fine large Death Cart by Lopez; a famous San Francisco; a fine flat style Madonna of the Rosary; and a carved staircase, carved mantels and arches from the Russell House in Providence.

*Connecticut.* MARINE HISTORICAL ASSOCIATION, MYSTIC.
Estimated total, 117. Boxes, 12; ship figureheads, 47; eagles, 6; ship gangway boards, 2; Indians, 1; ship stern decorations, 2; ship nameboards, lettered, 20; ship rudder decoration figure, 1; mirrors, 4; chairs, 16; miscellaneous, 4.
WADSWORTH ATHENEUM, HARTFORD.
Ship carving, 1; boxes, chests, chairs, 24; shop figures, 1; foot warmer, spoon rack, pipe box, 1 each; and numerous carved details on furniture.

*Delaware.* THE HENRY FRANCIS DU PONT WINTERTHUR MUSEUM, WINTERTHUR.
Estimated total, thousands.
DELAWARE STATE MUSEUM, DOVER.
Estimated total, 12.

*Illinois.* CHICAGO HISTORICAL SOCIETY, CHICAGO.
Estimated total, 24.

*Iowa.* NORWEGIAN-AMERICAN HISTORICAL MUSEUM, DECORAH.
Estimated total, 20.

*Louisiana.* LOUISIANA STATE MUSEUM, THE CABILDO, NEW ORLEANS.
Estimated total, 17.

*Massachusetts.* OLD STURBRIDGE VILLAGE, OLD STURBRIDGE.
Estimated total, 1500. Included are: boxes, 403; small boxes, 54;

Bible boxes, 6; desk boxes, 2; beds, 5; bookcases, 3; brackets (wall), 5; butter molds, 177; cases, 10; canes, 7; chests, 67; clocks, 25; chairs, 108; cupboards, 7; decoys, 35; desks, 10; dolls, 5; eagles, 35; fans, 3; fire screens, 2; mold and moldings, 15; nut crackers, 15; panels, 2; puppets, 8; racks, 23; rosaries, 2; shelves, 3; shoes, 3; sticks, 32; stands, 8; sofas, 1; tables, 53; toys, 55, whistles, 14.

THE BOSTONIAN SOCIETY, OLD STATE HOUSE, BOSTON.
Estimated total, 40. Including ship carvings, shop figures, architectural details, eagles, dolls and hobby horses.

MUSEUM OF FINE ARTS, BOSTON.
Numerous examples, especially in furniture carving.

WORCESTER ART MUSEUM.
Perhaps 10 pieces of carved furniture.

PEABODY MUSEUM, SALEM.
Estimated total, 790. Figureheads, sternboards, etc., 70; decoys, 20; scrimshaw (bone, ivory, wood), 700.

WORCESTER HISTORICAL SOCIETY, WORCESTER.
Estimated total, 310.

*Michigan.* THE EDISON INSTITUTE, DEARBORN.
Estimated total: Large quantities distributed in some 90 buildings. Including weathervanes, ship carvings, shop figures, cigar-store Indians, circus carvings, butter molds, toys and dolls.

*Minnesota.* MINNESOTA HISTORICAL SOCIETY, ST. PAUL.
Estimated total, 15.

*New Mexico.* MUSEUM OF INTERNATIONAL FOLK ART, SANTA FE.
Bultos, 12; furniture (various), 12; chairs, 11; benches, 5; tables, 6.

MUSEUM OF NEW MEXICO, PALACE OF GOVERNORS, SANTA FE.
Estimated total, 208. Corbels from old missions, 6; New Mexican bultos, 140; carved chests, 10; New Mexican chairs, 20; New Mexican benches, 10; U.S. Victorian parlor chairs, 10; New Mexican pine-chip-carved shutters, doors, grills, 6; cupboards, beds, grain tubs, 6.

*New York.* BROOKLYN MUSEUM, NEW YORK CITY.
Numerous examples in many categories, including: Architectural details, doors, furniture, eagles, textile printing blocks, butter molds, and many others.

METROPOLITAN MUSEUM OF ART, NEW YORK CITY.
Estimated total, several hundred. Including chiefly carved furniture, architectural treatments in individual period rooms and many fragments in cases, in storage and on loan.

NEW YORK HISTORICAL SOCIETY, NEW YORK CITY.
Estimated total, 75. Including eagles, weathervanes, ship carving, shop figures, carved chests, butter molds, toys, dolls, hobby horses.
NEW YORK STATE HISTORICAL ASSOCIATION. COOPERSTOWN, NEW YORK.
Estimated total, 70. Including bird sculpture, 17; figure sculpture, 13; ship carving, 6; toys, 6; trade signs, 5; weathervanes, 9; miscellaneous, 16.

*Pennsylvania* EVERHART MUSEUM OF NATURAL HISTORY, SCIENCE AND ART, SCRANTON.
Estimated total, 31.
BUCKS COUNTY HISTORICAL SOCIETY, DOYLESTOWN.
Estimated total, many. Shop figures, 21, and many others.
LANDIS VALLEY MUSEUM ASSOCIATION, LANCASTER.
Estimated total, many, including among others, riflestocks, 24; butter molds, 250; wood blocks, toys, shop figures, cake molds, figureheads, pipes, weathervanes, ships-in-bottles.

*Rhode Island.* KING PHILIP MUSEUM, HAFFENREFFER COLLECTION, MOUNT HOPE.
Estimated total, 200.
NEWPORT HISTORICAL SOCIETY, NEWPORT.
Estimated total, 24.
RHODE ISLAND SCHOOL OF DESIGN, MUSEUM OF ART, PROVIDENCE.
Estimated total, 150.

*Vermont.* SHELBURNE MUSEUM, SHELBURNE.
Estimated total, 320. Eagles, 42; weathervanes, 14; ship carvings, 7; shop figures, 45; circus carvings, 5; decoys, 23; toys, etc., 32; puppets, 18; dolls, 92.

*Virginia.* THE MARINERS' MUSEUM, NEWPORT NEWS.
Estimated total, 78. Figureheads, 20; ship nameboards, 23; pilothouse eagles, 5; paddlebox decorations, 3; stern decorations, 13; billetheads, 3; gangway boards, 5; miscellaneous, 7.

# SELECTED BIBLIOGRAPHY

ABRAHAM, EVELYN: "David G. Blythe, American Painter and Wood Carver" (1815–1865), *Antiques*, May 1935.

ADORJAN, LOUIS G.: Circus Exhibition in the Museum of the City of New York. MS (3 pp.) Research File, Index of American Design.

ALLEN, EDWARD B.: "Early American Carving," *International Studio*, May 1924.

AUSTIN, A. EVERETT JR.: The Museum of the American Circus. Sarasota, Florida (n.d.).

BARBEAU, MARIUS: *The Arts of French Canada*, 1613–1870. In Loan. Exhibition Catalog, 1946. The Detroit Institute of Arts.

————: "Notre Dame de Recouvrance," in *Les Archives de Folklore*, Ottawa, 1946, vol. 1. (See also Lasnier, Rina.)

BARBER, JOEL D.: *Wild Fowl Decoys*, Windward House, 1934.

BARNGROVER, C. M., AND BUTLIN, EARL: Circuses. MS Report, Iowa Unit (n.d.), Research File, Index of American Design.

BENTLEY, WILLIAM: *The Diary of William Bentley, D.D.*, Pastor of the East Church, Salem, Mass. The Essex Institute, Salem, Mass., 4 vols., 1905–1914.

BOYD, E.: *Saints and Saint Makers*, Laboratory of Anthropology, Santa Fe, New Mexico, 1946.

————: *Primitive American Art. Santos of New Mexico.* 1946. MS.

BROWN, M. L.: "John Welsh, Carver," *Antiques*, January 1926, p. 28.

CAHILL, HOLGER: "American Folk Art," *American Mercury*, September 1931.

————: American Folk Sculpture. In Newark Museum Catalog, October 1931–January 1932, pp. 39–46.

————: "You Can Trace the Roots of the American Style to America's Folk Art," *House Beautiful*, October 1950, p. 138.

CHAMBERLAIN, SAMUEL: *Salem Interiors*, Hastings House, New York, 1950.

CHRISTENSEN, ERWIN O.: *Popular Art in the United States*, Penguin Books (London), 1948.

————: *The Index of American Design*, The Macmillan Company, New York, 1950.

————: "Hail Columbia," *Antiques*, July 1949, p. 50.

————: "Justice," *Antiques*, January 1950, p. 56.

————: "A Symposium," *Antiques*, May 1950, pp. 355–362.

CORNELIUS, CHARLES O.: "Some Early American Doorways," Metropolitan Museum of Art *Bulletin*, October 1927.

CULVER, HENRY B.: "Private Collections of Ship Models" (Illustrations), *Antiques*, August 1923, p. 64ff. *Antiques*, September 1923, p. 125ff.

EVAN-THOMAS, OWEN: *Domestic Utensils of Wood*, XVI–XIX Century, O. Evan-Thomas, Ltd. (London), 1932.

FLOWER, MILTON E.: "Schimmel the Woodcarver," *Antiques*, October 1943, p. 164ff.

GARDNER, ALBERT TEN EYCK: *Yankee Stonecutters*, Columbia University Press, New York, 1945.

GRAHAM, JOHN M.: *Popular Art in America*, Brooklyn Museum Exhibition, 1939.

GREEN, SAMUEL M.: "Edbury Hatch: Down-East Carver," *Magazine of Art*, December 1948, p. 308.

HALPERT, EDITH G., AND COGAR, JAMES L.: *A Catalogue of the American Folk Art Collection of Colonial Williamsburg*, Williamsburg, Va., Colonial Williamsburg, 1947.

*Harper's Weekly:* January 6, 1883, p. 13.

HOUGHLAND, WILLARD: *Santos, A Primitive American Art Collection of Jan Kleijkamp and Ellis Monroe*, New York, 1946. Privately printed.

HOWELLS, JOHN MEAD: *The Architectural Heritage of the Merrimack*, Architectural Book Publishing Company, Inc., New York, 1941.

————: *The Architectural Heritage of the Piscataqua*, Architectural Book Publishing Company, Inc., New York, 1937.

HYNSON, GARRET, AND NASH, SUSAN HIGGINSON: "Design in Yankee Butter Molds," *Antiques*, February 1942, pp. 131–133.

JESSUP, L. F.: "Tobacconists' Tribe of Treen," *Antiques*, September 1930, pp. 232–235.

JONES, BARBARA: *The Unsophisticated Arts*, The Architectural Press, Rochester, Kent (England), 1951.

JONES, LOUIS C.: "The Folk Art Collection," *Art in America*, April 1950, pp. 109–123.

KETTELL, RUSSELL HAWES: *The Pine Furniture of Early New England*, Dover Publications, Inc., New York, 1929.

KIMBALL, FISKE: *Mr. Samuel McIntire, Carver, the Architect of Salem*, The Southworth-Anthoensen Press, Portland, Me., 1940.

————: *Domestic Architecture of the American Colonies and of the Early Republic*, Charles Scribner's Sons, New York, 1927.

LARSEN, PETER: "Butter Stamps and Molds," *Antiques*, July 1939, pp. 29–30.

LASNIER, RINA, AND BARBEAU, MARIUS: *Madonnes Canadiennes*, Montreal, 1944.

LAUGHTON, L. G. CARR: *Old Ship Figure-Heads and Their Sterns*, Hatton & Smith (London), 1925.

LICHTEN, FRANCES: *Folk Art of Rural Pennsylvania*, Charles Scribner's Sons, New York, 1946.

LIPMAN, JEAN: *American Folk Art in Wood, Metal and Stone*, Pantheon, New York, 1948.

LORD DEXTER OF NEWBURYPORT: "The Voice of the People," *Antiques*, March 1923, pp. 107–108.

McCAUSLAND, ELIZABETH: "A Selected Bibliography on American Painting and Sculpture from the Colonial Times to the Present," *Magazine of Art*, November 1946, p. 329ff.

MANGRAVITE, PEPPINO: "Saints and a Death Angel," *Magazine of Art*, March 1940, pp. 160–165.

MARCEAU, HENRI: *William Rush*, Philadelphia Museum Catalogue, 1937.

MICHEL, ANDRÉ: *Histoire de l'Art*, A. Colin, Paris, 1905–1929, Vol. VI, 2, 1922.

MILLER, DOROTHY: *The Life and Work of David G. Blythe*, University of Pittsburgh Press, 1950.

MORRISON, J. L.: "Passing of the Wooden Indian," *Scribners Magazine*, October 1928, pp. 393–405.

*Notes on American Carvers and Carving.* Report, April 1938. MS (Compilation). Research File, Index of American Design.

PINCKNEY, PAULINE A.: *American Figureheads and Their Carvers*, W. W. Norton & Company, New York, 1940.

RICHARDSON, E. P.: *The Arts of French Canada*, 1613–1870. Loan Exhibition Catalogue, The Detroit Institute of Arts, 1946.

ROBINSON, ELINOR: *American Folk Sculpture*, Newark Museum Catalogue, October 1931–January 1932.

ROSENWALD, JANET: *American Figureheads.* Report, November 26, 1937, March 1938. MS. Research Files, Index of American Design.

ROURKE, CONSTANCE: *The Roots of American Culture*, Harcourt, Brace & Company, 1942.

SACK, ALBERT: *Fine Points of Furniture, Early American*, Crown Publishers, New York, 1950.

SANBORN, KATE: *Hunting Indians in a Taxicab*, Gorham Press, Boston, 1911.

*Scientific American:* "The Figurehead and Its Story," August 7, 1909, p. 92ff (Ill. p. 93).

SHAW, CHARLES G.: "Speaking of Wooden Indians," *Antiques*, September 1939, p. 131.
———: "Black Boys and Their Playfellows," *Antiques*, March 1934, p. 101.

STAFFORD, VICTOR: "John Haley Bellamy," *Antiques*, March 1935, pp. 102–107.

Swan, Mabel M.: Articles in *Antiques*, December 1931, p. 342; March 1948, p. 198.

*Tobacco* and the *Tobacco News;* An Illustrated Journal: New York, April 8, 1887, p. 2. "The Tobacconist's Sign."

Waterman, Thomas T.: *The Dwellings of Colonial America*, University of North Carolina Press, Chapel Hill, 1950.

Watson, Edith S., and Hayward, Victoria: "Figureheads of the Old Squareriggers" (Illustrations), *Century Magazine*, August 1916, pp. 566–573.

Weitenkampf, Frank W.: "Lo, The Wooden Indian," *The New York Times*, August 3, 1890, p. 13.
————: "Cigarstore Indians," *Magazine of Art*, December 1948, p.

312.

Whitehall, Virginia A.: "American Circus Carvings," *Magazine of Art*, 1943, pp. 172–175.

Wilder, Mitchell A., and Breitenbach, Edgar: *Santos, The Religious Folk Art of New Mexico*, The Taylor Museum, Colorado Springs Fine Arts Center, Colorado, 1943.

# INDEX

145